MY MANTELPIECE

My Mantelpiece

a memoir of survival
and social justice

Carolyn Goodman
with Brad Herzog

FOREWORD BY **MAYA ANGELOU**

Why Not Books
831 Spruce Avenue
Pacific Grove, CA 93950
www.WhyNotBooks.com

ISBN 978-0-9849919-4-5
Library of Congress Control Number: 2013955857
First edition: May 2014

Book design by Tessa Avila
Edited by Eric Braun
Copyedited by John Deever
Cover photo by John Abbott
Photo p. 196 credit: Fred R. Conrad / The New York Times / Redux

10 9 8 7 6 5 4 3 2 1

Printed with soy inks

Printed in the United States of America

ALSO BY BRAD HERZOG

States of Mind

Small World

Turn Left at the Trojan Horse

*This book is dedicated to the memory of Carolyn Goodman,
who gave me the honor of listening and learning as she revealed
her story over the course of many hours, days, and weeks before
she passed away. On subjects both intimate and epic, she told her
tale candidly, unflinchingly, and profoundly in the belief that the
lessons of her life would survive long after her death.*

BRAD HERZOG

CONTENTS

Foreword by Maya Angelou   1

THE MANTELPIECE   7

LETTING HIM GO   9

PIECES OF ME   19

A Child of Hope   32

THE COMPANY OF MEN   33

DISTANCE   45

Melodies Unheard   56

THE POET AND THE SWORD   57

ONE ARM OVER THE OTHER   71

Tupper Lake   80

A BAR OF CONTENTMENT IN A SEA OF SONG   81

THE ZEST OF THEIR LEAPING EYES   91

Letter from Philadelphia   117

FOOTSTEPS   119

A SHORT WHILE TOWARDS THE SUN   131

The Equation of Life   149

SAVING MYSELF   151

JUSTICE   175

Fling Stars   138

NO TWILIGHT   139

Remembrance   197

FOREWORD

$\mathcal{C}$arolyn Goodman and I liked each other very much. We just admired each other. Beyond that, there was affection. But there was admiration, too, because each knew who the other one was. I knew she was a strong and loving woman. And she knew I was the same. Some people can be strong without love, and some can have love without strength. So they can't encourage people to go further, to be more ambitious. Love is such a wonderful encouragement. It's not just a feeling. It may be that which keeps the stars in the firmament.

So I liked her and loved her.

The murders of Andrew Goodman, James Chaney, and Mickey Schwerner rocked me to the core of my very being. I had grown up in a little village in Arkansas. Lynchings were not unusual. And they were legal, as far as we could see. Nobody ever went to jail for them. So I was used to white men killing black men. But I was not used to white men killing white men because of black men.

The difference! It was almost as if, in the former, they had license to kill black men. This is what they did. The KKK did that. They killed black men in various murderous ways. But killing young white men? I thought, *These people are really mad!* It was amazing to me. I had to look at the murderers with different eyes. It rocked me.

For a few hundred years, white men could order black men to do anything, and they had to do it—including die. They could order black women to do anything, and they had to do it, which explains so many light-skinned black people. But all white men were free. Even indentured servants were free in that they could write to somebody in the country they came from and get some sort of help. If they were brought here from England, they could always write back. England was there. But the black man and black woman had no place to call to, to write to, to ask for succor, sustenance, support.

It seemed that white men had no say over other white men. And in fact, white men tried to make friends with other white men so that they could have some support in what they did. They had allies. The first thing the white man had to do was convince himself that the black man deserved slavery. And the second thing he had to do was convince his friends, his allies, that the black man deserved slavery, so that he could have some support.

So those murders in 1964 were shocking. And I felt for the mothers of the white boys. You see, the mother of a black boy knows that when he leaves home, she may never see him again, no matter where. But the white mother didn't know that.

Those three young men represent three hundred thousand young men and women who dared, who had the courage to go to the lion's den and try to scrub the lion's teeth. People live in direct relation to the heroes and she-roes that they have, always and always. Young people can look at the famous football player, the well-known baseball player, the golfer and say, "I want to be like that." Well, we have to have that in the civil rights movement. Some became famous because of what they said. We have to have the people who became famous for what they did. And I think those three are unmitigated heroes, so we have to lift them up and show them to the world, so that some young man in Philadelphia or Tucson, Arizona, says, "I wonder, could I stand up for Right even though it doesn't actually concern me?" Not knowing that by standing up for Right, he's actually doing the right thing for himself.

DR. MAYA ANGELOU
October 2013

MY MANTELPIECE

THE MANTELPIECE

*W*hen my youngest son David was seven years old, he came running home from school one day, breathless with excitement. In his hands he held a large piece of construction paper smothered in assorted colors, lines, shapes, and squiggles. In the eyes of a seven-year-old, it was a creation of unmatched brilliance, Monet and Degas and O'Keeffe all rolled into one. In fact, that's quite literally what it looked like.

With the flamboyance only a true artist can exude, David boomed into our Upper West Side apartment, raised his magnum opus, and proudly declared, "Mom, come here! Look at my mantelpiece!"

The story always made me smile. I treasured it and retold it because it evoked so much through so little. The exuberance of youth. The humor of language. The wonder of artistry. The power of approval. That David, perhaps trying to approximate the speech of his parents or the growing vocabulary of his older brothers, would substitute "mantelpiece" for "masterpiece" seems as profound as it is comical. The mantelpiece, after all, is where we keep our most prized creations, the photos and collectibles of loved ones and watershed moments. It is where we put our past and future on display. It is a self-portrait through faces and places, the *me* that we choose to show the world. A masterpiece is essentially the product of another's estimation. Someone else reviews your life's work and pronounces judgment. But a mantelpiece is a personal statement of values and choices, your life's work presented as a museum of the self.

I have chosen to put mine into words, primarily because I believe lessons are the harvest of a lifetime, and I feel as if I have lived a hundred lifetimes. I loved deeply, lost horribly, explored curiously. I surrendered friends to political paranoia, husbands to illness, a father to depression, and a son to hatred. I befriended icons, met presidents, fought fascists, found heroes. I was a victim and an inspiration, a martyr and an activist, a doctor and a patient. I mourned and celebrated and strayed and achieved and learned.

My life has been a work of art—a wondrous, colorful, tragic, flawed, intimate and epic work of art. This is my story. This is my mantelpiece.

LETTING HIM GO

$\mathcal{O}$n my mantelpiece sits a photograph of a young man with thick, wavy black hair and eyes dark with the depth of understanding. It is Andy, my middle son. My oldest son, Jonathan, and my youngest, David, both look like me. But Andy was the image of his father, Bobby. He had his father's walk, his father's hands, his hair, his mouth, his soft brown eyes. His whole face had a soft quality to it, but there was an intensity of purpose behind it. Every time I looked at the photo of that face, which was often, I thought of the last time I saw it.

Like his father, Andy was the kind of person who didn't harbor malice. If he was angry, you knew it. If he was sad, he showed it. There was an honesty about him that allowed a remarkable range of emotion. However, being the middle son,

Andy always seemed to play the role of the mediator. When Jonathan and David would argue, it would be Andy who would intervene. There was something soothing about his demeanor, something mature about his judgment. I remember a particular incident in school, for example. One of his classmates, despite being very small for his age, always seemed to pick on bigger kids, possibly because he felt so insecure himself. One day, several classmates cornered the kid, piled on top of him, and started to beat on him. When Andy walked by, he pulled them off of the boy. He was always strong, but I was more impressed by his strength of character. It was just like him to intervene. "Look," he told his classmates, "I know Joey's a pest. But one at a time. It's only fair."

When Andy was a child, Jackie Robinson was his hero. It was typical. We lived closer to the Bronx than to Brooklyn. Andy had plenty of glittering Yankees to choose from. Yogi Berra. Mickey Mantle. Whitey Ford. Instead, he chose one of the underdog Dodgers: a pioneer, an activist, someone who knew the burden of representing more than just himself. When he learned that Jackie lived only a few blocks from his school, Andy asked him to come speak to his classmates. And Jackie did. Andy became as much a hero to his classmates as Jackie. That was typical, too. Andy wasn't an aggressive person in any sense of the word, but as his paternal grandfather would say, he was a doer. You don't just talk; you do. That was Andy.

He was an activist all of his life. At age fifteen, he traveled to Washington D.C., for a Youth March for Integrated Schools. At seventeen, he and a friend journeyed to West Virginia by bus to examine firsthand the poverty of Appalachia. At nineteen, he took a job as a summer counselor at a camp for underprivileged children. Then, in the spring of 1964, he stood in the doorway of my bedroom one afternoon with an earnest look in his soft brown eyes and said, "Mom, I'd like to go to Mississippi."

The Mississippi Summer Project, as they called it, was an effort by the Council of Federated Organizations to flood the state with hundreds of northern college students. The volunteers would form "freedom schools" to teach disenfranchised blacks about their constitutional rights and would engage in a massive voter registration drive. *The New York Times* called it "one of the most ambitious civil rights projects yet conceived," but many people involved with the project, we later discovered, secretly believed that the inevitable violence against these so-called Yankee do-gooders would direct the nation's attention to the intolerable conditions in the state. It was a recipe for martyrdom.

In the previous seven decades, nearly six hundred known lynchings had taken place in the state—the most in the nation. The violence against blacks had been particularly staggering in the ten years since the U.S. Supreme Court's *Brown v. Board of Education* decision. Having been told that separate is inherently unequal, Mississippi had simply become more entrenched.

I remembered a horrific event that had happened when Andy was eleven, the murder of Emmett Till, a fourteen-year-old boy on vacation from Chicago who reportedly whistled at a young white woman in a store deep in the Delta. Three days later, his body was found in the Tallahatchie River. Barbed wire had been used to tie a cotton gin fan to his neck. His killers were acquitted by an all-white jury. Two weeks earlier, a black man named Lamar Smith who had organized blacks to vote in a recent election had been shot dead by a white assailant in broad daylight while dozens of people watched. The killer was never indicted because no one would admit to seeing a white man shoot a black man.

I recalled the case of Mack Charles Parker, a twenty-three-year-old black man accused of raping a white woman. Three days before his case was set for trial, a masked mob took him from his jail cell, beat him, shot him, wrapped him in chains, and threw him in the Pearl River. The local law enforcement apparently was aware of every move. The men were never convicted. Two years later, Herbert Lee was murdered by a state legislator for working to register black voters. Louis Allen, a black man who witnessed the crime, endured several years of arrests and threats. On the day he was making final arrangements to move north and away from that hateful place, he too was killed.

And, of course, I knew about Medgar Evers, the NAACP field secretary and patron saint of the civil rights movement in

Mississippi, who told a crowd in 1963, "I love my children, and I love my wife with all my heart. And I would die, and die gladly, if that would make a better life for them." Five days later, he was shot in his driveway, collapsing near a pile of shirts he was carrying that read "Jim Crow Must Go." An outspoken member of the White Citizens' Council was arrested for the murder. The murder weapon was registered to him and held his fingerprints. Several witnesses testified that he had asked directions to Evers's home. It took three decades to convict him.

Even then, the names of the towns were like dark bruises on my memory. Money, Mississippi. Poplarville, Mississippi. Jackson, Mississippi. Liberty, Mississippi. I couldn't help it. The Deep South put fear in my heart in 1964. Mississippi was a terrifying word.

That was where my son was asking permission to go. A place still twenty-two years away from electing its first post-Reconstruction black congressman, twenty-three years from removing a ban on interracial marriage from its constitution, and thirty-one years from actually ratifying the federal constitutional amendment outlawing slavery. A state with a chief executive, Governor Ross Barnett, who physically blocked the integration of the University of Mississippi after claiming, "The Negro is different because God made him different to punish him." And in the terrible words of many Mississippians themselves, the only thing worse than a nigger was a nigger lover.

But the reasons why part of me so wanted Andy to stay were the same reasons he wanted to go. The state with the largest percentage of blacks in the country had the lowest percentage of black voters. Only five percent of Mississippi's half a million African-Americans were registered to vote in 1960. In eight of the state's thirteen mostly black counties, not a single African-American citizen had ever voted. My son wanted to be a beacon of light in the heart of darkness. How could I deny him?

Only a couple of years earlier, Andy had been helping his father as a laborer on the Alexander Hamilton Bridge, which spans the Harlem River. He was working there one day when he heard a shout and turned to see a man holding on by his fingertips. He was a heavy man, a black man named Roosevelt. He had slipped and was clinging to the side of the bridge. Andy rushed over and, mustering all his strength, grabbed him and pulled him to safety. It was a physical feat, less courageous than instinctive. But looking back, it seems like such a metaphorical message. Andy's desire to head south was just as instinctive, perhaps more courageous, similarly warranted. Essentially, it was a grander, more figurative attempt to pull others to safety. Andy risked his life saving one man. Why not do the same to save thousands?

I suppose my past flashed before my eyes, too—growing up during the women's suffrage movement, organizing on behalf of dairy farmers during the Depression, joining the fight against Spanish fascism, protecting friends from the McCarthy witch hunt. I had fought for what I had believed in. I had found and loved a husband who had done the same, fostering in me a greater sense of the greater good. It could be that I thought back to the tragedy of my own parents—a mother devoid of compassion, a father lacking fortitude—and embraced the notion that my son was a spiritual reflection of myself.

Bobby and I later realized there was no way in the world we could have said no to Andy. Our lives, our values, would have had a hollow ring. While Bobby was away building whirler cranes that repaired ships in the navy yard in Philadelphia during World War II, he had written a sweet, poetic note to me. Bobby was a civil engineer for a living, but he was always a poet at heart. This particular letter referred to our then-one-year-old son, Andy. "Teach our son to tread softly," he wrote, "and make his walk through the woods . . . of this world the symphony of our dreams." But because Andy was, indeed, the symphony of our dreams, his will would not allow him to tread softly.

There again, he was his father's son. Nearly three decades earlier, when he, too, was a twenty-year-old with so much of the world on fire, Bobby won an oratorical award at Cornell University for a speech titled "A Plea for Active Pacifism." He spoke these words: "Sometimes, even if he must do it alone and his conduct seems mad, a man must set an example and draw out men's souls from the mire of the swamp, and spur them on by some act of righteous indignation that this great idea may not die."

But Bobby wasn't home on that spring morning in 1964 when Andy, standing in the doorway, said, "Mom, I'd like to go to Mississippi."

As thousands of thoughts raced through my mind, I could only stammer, "Let's wait for your dad to come home."

Other parents refused their underage children permission, but I just couldn't deny him. I wanted him to go, and I didn't want him to go. Here was my son, whom I wanted to protect and save from anything hurtful, and yet it wouldn't have felt right saying, *Well, let the other guys go, but don't you go.* It would have destroyed our values. It would have devastated our son. Bobby later gave Andy the answer I knew he would.

As Andy was preparing to leave, having packed his duffel bag, I threw in some bandages, gauze, and iodine when he walked out of the room. I knew where he was going. I knew he would become intensely involved, as he always did. I thought he might get pushed around a bit, perhaps even thrown in jail. Never in my wildest dreams did I think this would be the last time I would see him.

We stood in my study in the apartment eight floors above West Eighty-sixth Street. It is the same study I used for another four decades. It didn't change much over the years, although, of course, everything around it did. When I hugged my son for the last time, perhaps I gripped him a little harder than usual. Maybe I looked at his face a little longer. Andy seemed so young, so strong, so beautiful. He had just turned twenty. He will always be twenty to me.

And I said goodbye.

There are forty names inscribed on the Civil Rights Memorial in Montgomery, Alabama, names of people who died during the struggle in the years between the *Brown* decision and Martin Luther King's death. Of the forty victims, nineteen were killed in Mississippi. One of them is my son.

I allowed him to go there, and I was both guilt-ridden and proud, and I devoted the rest of my life to making sure he did not die in vain. I permitted him to go to Mississippi because that is who he was. And it is who I was, too.

PIECES OF ME

*T*he socks. I always remembered the socks.

Maybe it was simply the distraction, or perhaps the lack of abstraction. It was something fixed on which I could focus for a few moments while the rest of my world seemed to spin out of control. Maybe it was the sheer repetition of the act, over and over again until it was seared into my fragile psyche. My later psychological training would reveal how the brain can attach profound significance to certain objects during times of overwhelming emotion. But I was five years old. All I knew was that my brother, my playmate, my protector had been taken from me in the blink of an eye.

For some reason, the traumatic moments that would have been so vivid amid the tragedy didn't linger in my memory.

There must have been an anxious drive to the emergency room, a turn for the worse, frantic nurses rushing by, an interminable wait, a somber doctor, a gasp, perhaps a sobbing collapse to the cold hospital floor. There must have been a funeral. Those recollections were lost in the haze. But not the socks.

Was it a few days after Eddie died? Was it weeks later? My mother sat on my bed, straight-backed, laundry by her side. She picked up one small sock, searched vacant-eyed for a moment, found a match, and silently rolled them up together. Then she did it again and again, two by two by two, as the tears flowed down her cheeks. Just rolling socks and crying, rolling and crying, rolling and crying. I sat next to her, mesmerized. It was the first time that I could ever recall seeing tears in my mother's eyes. Perhaps the last time, too.

Looking back, maybe I sensed a certain symbolism in the need to pair them up. One sock is useless, abandoned, discarded. And that's my other recollection.

I dimly recall a procession of mourners arriving at the big house in Far Rockaway, New York. I sat by the window and watched as they trudged up the steps of the wraparound porch, paused uncomfortably for a moment, adopted what they felt was an appropriate expression of condolence, then rang the doorbell. Several of the women carried dishes—cakes and casseroles and such—and I thought it seemed like such a strange tradition. As if we were sad because we were hungry.

The whisper of voices in the dining room and living room soon grew in volume, and as I stared up at the men holding their hats and the women in their black dresses, I caught snippets of talk about inconsequential things. *Why isn't anybody discussing it? Eddie died. Don't they know?* Soon, the doorbell didn't ring anymore. The door was left unlocked. People simply walked in, somewhat haltingly, yet as if they had been expected. It all seemed so unnatural.

Come in, come in. Don't talk about it. Come in.

Once in a while, someone would notice me. They would smile sadly or place a light hand on my shoulder, and then they would turn their attention to the sponge cake or the tuna casserole or the neighbor from down the street who suddenly required an immediate handshake. Maybe they didn't know what to say to me, or they thought that I couldn't fully comprehend the situation, or they feared I was too fragile for condolences. Maybe,

Eddie and Carolyn Drucker, 1913

conversely, they figured children are resilient. Surely, they had their reasons. But I felt very much alone, like a single sock.

It is ironic, of course, that over the ensuing generations my life was so often defined by my response to the death of a loved one. Later, I ultimately chose to confront hurt rather than be overwhelmed by it. Yet in this, the first loss of so many, some of my earliest memories are of people wishing to avoid the subject altogether.

$\mathscr{I}$n nine decades of observing, a lifetime of analyzing and hypothesizing and extrapolating, I did not learn one damn thing about the meaning of life. Frankly, I never quite came to the conclusion that there is such a thing. But it was not the meaning of life that interested me anyway; it was the meaning of people. Through my years as a daughter, wife, and mother, through my efforts as a psychologist and an activist, I often wondered: What are the roots and influences that form a person? What makes us . . . us?

I concluded that each of us is a puzzle of sorts, a collection of interconnected pieces, some larger than others, some more obvious, all of which interlock to form the complete person. Each of the puzzle pieces is a part of the origin of ourselves.

Are we reflections of our era, for instance? My generation was born during the first "Great War," came of age during the Depression, had children during World War II, raised those children amid the specter of McCarthyism, and watched them mature amid the upheaval of the Sixties. To what extent are we the amalgam or residue of shared general experience? Then again, what role does one's environment play in the development of one's character and outlook? Where we live, whom we encounter, the myriad events and settings that constitute our personal experience—we mold them, they influence us. It is a circular process, perhaps one without a definable beginning.

Certainly, two large pieces are represented by our ancestry—our cultural surroundings, our traditions, the people who may have left the original footprints along the path we now take—and, of course, our parents, puzzling though they can be. As I learned through personal and professional experience, creation of a person does not end with conception. We are inevitably the product of our parenting, whether good, bad or indifferent.

Each of the parts fits together differently for each person. Some pieces loom large, some are difficult to connect, some may be missing altogether. The meaning of people is an unsolved puzzle. I can only approach the answer by exploring my own origins, my own influences, the pieces of me.

You could say freedom spawned me. It is as good a place as any to begin. My great-grandparents on both sides arrived in New York City following a long escape from persecution. My mother's grandparents, Casper and Esther Fisher, came from Alsace-Lorraine on the French-German border, one of those slices of land in the world that changed hands often. The loss of religious and political freedom that followed the German Revolution had sent thousands of Central European immigrants to America in the middle of the nineteenth century. My ancestors were among them.

My father's family was rooted in Western Europe until the Spanish Inquisition sent them scrambling for a safe haven. In a series of events not unlike those unleashed by Hitler's regime nearly five centuries later, Spanish Jews were targets of fanatical anti-Semite Tomas de Torquemada's wrath, in part because they had risen to such high positions in finance, commerce, medicine, and local government. Some one hundred thousand of them were murdered, tortured, or imprisoned. In 1492, the same year King Ferdinand and Queen Isabella financed the voyage of Columbus, they were persuaded to expel all Jews who refused to be baptized in a Christian ceremony. That the Inquisition led my ancestors to Holland and eventually to America, where many of my Jewish friends and I later would join the fight against Spanish fascism, is a case of delicious historical irony.

My maiden name, Drucker, was originally spelled Drooker. That's Dutch for "printer," which was the family business somewhere along the line. The Druckers arrived in Manhattan in the 1840s. I never knew my paternal grandfather. He died before I was born. I barely knew my grandmother, who died soon after. My mother was not all that anxious to visit her mother-in-law, so we didn't, and thus my paternal grandmother never was a significant part of my life. I don't even recall her name.

There was always, however, a vague recollection, the kind that makes one question whether the memory is sparked by a photograph or by legitimate recall. Funny how that happens, how snapshots and heirlooms and stories told and retold become the backbone of our remembrances. Do the snapshots exist because they were moments worth capturing? Are the heirlooms made weighty by the hands that have touched them? Do oft-told tales merit their repetition? Or are they all just lifelines to prevent us from drowning in the things we have forgotten? I often wondered. Nevertheless, I long held onto a vision of my grandmother—a very nice-looking woman with her gray hair piled on top of her head—and I cherished that vision, regardless of its origin.

Although the Druckers probably could be classified as lower middle class, my father, Edward, worked diligently, entered New York Law School, passed the bar, and became a lawyer in Manhattan. His success personified the American Dream—the son of an immigrant family turning a mostly free education into a career as a big-city attorney. And he loved the country that gave him that opportunity.

My mother, Ruth, on the other hand, took all that she could and gave back little. Her parents had money, her father having become wealthy as a manufacturer of denim jeans. They lived at the location of what is now the Majestic Apartments on Seventy-second Street and Central Park West. At the time, it was the Majestic Hotel. They lived on the top floor. The Fishers sent Ruth to Barnard College, and she soon dropped out. It wasn't because she couldn't make the grade. She was brilliant. But she just didn't care.

Ruth Fisher and Edward Drucker met in Long Branch, New Jersey, where the Fishers owned a beautiful summer home. During one of my mother's frequent summers there, a mutual friend told her of a handsome young man she wanted her to meet. And, indeed, he was a fine physical match for my mother. Maybe they were even in love at first. Romance has a way of blooming so beautifully before it recedes with the cold of resignation and regret. He was in his late twenties; she was in her early twenties. It was the peak of their relationship.

They were married in 1912, and their first child, a son, was born one year later. One is not supposed to name a Jewish child after living parents, but my mother named him Edward anyway. She cared little about religious customs or, for that matter, customs of any kind. At the time, it must have seemed quaint and sentimental, but later events just redefined it as morbid and telling. I think, in my mother's eyes, my father died long before he killed himself.

$\mathcal{I}$ was born at a time when the world was changing dramatically. In my infancy, the first air conditioners and traffic lights were invented. Einstein published his theory of relativity. Charlie Chaplin unveiled the Little Tramp. Babe Ruth was a rookie. But with change also came the threat of war, and I arrived quite auspiciously and quite literally amid the fear and intolerance that stemmed from that threat. It was 1915, and as Russia and France battled German forces across the ocean, the United States remained neutral in name only. Anti-German sentiment was already entrenched. The German Hospital at Seventy-seventh Street and Park Avenue soon succumbed, changing its name to Lenox Hill Hospital, even though about ninety-five percent of the doctors and nurses there spoke German. On October 6, five months after the sinking of the Lusitania, I was born there.

Like my sons after me, my earliest childhood was dominated by world war. History will judge whether it was a battle for economic and political advantage or, in Woodrow Wilson's words, a fight "to make the world safe for democracy." They called it the war to end all wars. God knows it certainly wasn't. I have no recollection of the war, nor even of the apartment my family rented on St. Nicholas Avenue in a middle-class Jewish community that is now part of Harlem. But I do recall the marble steps one had to climb to reach the apartment, and I distinctly remember sitting there with my mother, sometimes talking, sometimes listening enraptured as she read to me. I can only wonder, with no small sense of irony, why my memories begin there, with my mother mothering.

Our family made its way to Long Island when I was three, to Far Rockaway in Queens, which was then considered the country. My mother was none too excited about moving away from the city, away from her parents, to a place where the distractions were fewer. We moved again within a couple of years to what seemed like an enormous house, also in Far Rockaway, a house that my grandfather helped purchase. When you're a child, everything seems outsized. But this was big. It had a basement and three floors—a kitchen, dining room, and living room on the first floor, bedrooms on the second floor, and an attic at the top. It had the red-shingled feel of a country home with that

Carolyn Drucker, age 5

large, wraparound porch. The milkman and ice wagon used to deliver daily, their horses' hooves clattering down my block. When it was very cold in the winter, I would stand on the heating grates on the floor in search of warmth.

Within my family, I found little of the warmth I so desperately sought. My father was working every day, commuting into New York City, returning home to his books and his garden. Oh, how he loved that garden. He grew grapes, which I always associated with a peculiar memory: I was walking home from school one day, probably in second or third grade, when in horror I watched a car run over and kill a cat that had been scurrying across the street. I sprinted the rest of the way home, harboring a vision that this cat wasn't really dead. For a while, in fact, I had nightmares that this cat was bloodied and running after me. (We always had dogs around the house—one of whom, Laddy, was also run over by an ice truck, a very sad day in my life—but I never liked cats, and that particular one always haunted me). When my father returned home that evening, I told him about the accident. He grabbed a shovel, found the cat, and buried it beneath his grape arbor—as fertilizer, I imagine.

I never forgot that incident. For a good twenty years, I avoided grapes. And I was never crazy about wine.

So my father's care for his garden was evidence of his tender heart. My mother, however, was distant. Intelligent, willful, often generous, but distant. My brother Eddie, older by two years, was my chief source of happiness. I tagged along with him constantly, always at his heels. Sometimes he didn't object, sometimes he found me a pain in the neck, but always he was the one person with whom I felt safe—until he was gone. Just like that.

Septicemia, they called it. I later looked it up in the dictionary. A systematic disease caused by pathogenic organisms or their toxins in the bloodstream. First he had suffered a terrible pain in his abdomen. By the time they took him to the hospital his appendix had burst. And then he disappeared. He just wasn't there. And soon, it felt as if I wasn't there either. Nobody talked to me about it. My mother didn't say a word to me in that moment, as she paired the socks. It was as if the sorrow was hers only. My father may not have been prepared to handle the task of addressing my devastation while being so immersed in his own.

I suppose that may be the reason I always tried to be open with my children through tragedy and triumph, about the events that shaped all of us. In part, I regretted not knowing much about my own family history. I didn't feel as if I had been bolstered by ancestral tales, which might have shaped me. And although I would mature into womanhood during the Depression, I wasn't affected by it. As a child, at least, the seminal events of my era were more distant headlines than intimate influences. I felt somewhat confused by a changing environment, a bit removed from my family. I wasn't made to feel like a piece of an interconnected puzzle.

In the end, however, I realized that it didn't really matter how the various pieces of me fit together because we are never fully formed. We live—and hopefully breathe—deeply. We interpret our experiences, knowing that truth is perception, and in doing so we add layers to ourselves. Life is not a passive experience. I vowed to take action.

A CHILD OF HOPE

A poet is a child of hope

Not a prophet of despair

That clings to the edge of fear.

He tugs at your soul, your heart

Or whatever the symbol of you—

You choose to think that part

Of yourself that keeps up

When the sun is golden in the West,

And a tinge of your hope becomes

A dream in the spangled sky.

A poet is a man of phantom,

That toys with gloom

Like a kitten with a dangling cord.

A puppeteer of the heartstring

Subservient to the echo of your need

So well does he catch the signal of his own.

—Bobby Goodman

THE COMPANY OF MEN

We had a beautiful, expansive lawn on the side of our house, and my father meticulously cared for it. He pulled weeds, he kept it trimmed and edged, and he watered and fertilized it regularly. But one day he returned from a long day at the office to find it not so beautiful. The grass was trampled and muddy with divots and footprints.

"What happened here?" he asked, as he stood in the living room and turned his attention from the window to me.

"I was playing football," I told him, "with the boys."

His face reddened. His eyes narrowed. "You were what?"

I looked at the ground, avoiding his gaze. The lawn was his pride and joy. How could I have been so careless? But what he said next surprised me.

"Don't you ever dare do that again! Girls don't play such games."

And here I thought it was the condition of the lawn that bothered him. The very next night he came home with knitting needles and yarn and told me it was time I learned how to knit. And I did. I sat there properly with the needle in my right hand and the yarn in my left, and I looped and stitched and made afghans and sweaters. And I behaved like a little lady. And it pleased my father. And it was all a charade.

Eddie had been my social conduit to the boys. He hung around with them; I tagged along. His presence had protected me from my own confusion about who I wanted to be—and with whom. I remember wandering around behind my house and feeling very much alone, once again, less because the others did not want to be with me than because I preferred being by myself.

Soon, I realized that it wasn't actually solitude that I preferred. It was simply that I was repelled by the traditional role I was expected to play, like the title character in *Rebecca of Sunnybrook Farm,* a book that was already a classic even when I was a little girl. From the time I was very little, I found men much more interesting than women. As fate would have it, eventually I would have two husbands, three sons, and a psychosexual fascination with the male gender. But as a child, I simply became a tomboy. I loved boys and loved the things that boys did. The rough-and-tumble games. Their permission to be more active, more spontaneous, and to express themselves more openly. I wanted to be a part of that.

A couple of girls lived on my block, but I never had much fun with them. I found them dull, restrained, and restricted by traditional role-playing. Primarily middle-class girls, their lives consisted of a series of admonitions: You don't do this, and you don't do that. If you did it, you didn't talk about it. And if you didn't do it, you probably wished you had.

All that despite it being a time of terrific achievement in the fight for women's rights. When I was five, the Nineteenth Amendment finally gave women the right to vote. When I was six, Margaret Sanger founded the American Birth Control League. When I was eight, the first Equal Rights Amendment was proposed. I heard about but did not quite understand these rumblings of a women's revolution. What does a little kid know of suffrage and sexual mores? For me, landmark national events hardly existed in comparison with a mother's comportment. Most of the girls I knew seemed to have traditional mothers. I did not. My mother cut her hair before it was fashionable. She didn't particularly care how she dressed. She did not wear a bra, nor did she keep house or cook. And she was not especially nurturing. Yet no sense of activism made Ruth Drucker frown upon tradition; as with so many other things, she just did as she pleased. Maybe my mother's disdain for convention opened my eyes to alternative possibilities. Perhaps it was ingrained in me from the beginning. Regardless, I was a girl yearning for a boy's way of life.

The consistent conflict between my preferences and society's expectations came to a head that evening with the trampled lawn. I suspect that when my father later caught sight of me knitting while the boys were out tackling each other he may have briefly enjoyed creating the kind of woman he wished my mother had been.

*C*urious as always, when I was still quite young, still living in Far Rockaway, I asked my mother a simple question: "Do you love Daddy?" Even at that age, I must have sensed something lacking in their relationship. She turned to me and gave me a quizzical look that I never forgot.

"Love?" she replied. "That's hard to answer."

And that was that.

Carolyn with her father and mother

Maybe that's why she seemed to try to sabotage the life and the family that they had made together. Maybe that's why she lost—if she ever really had it—any real identification with her parents' class and instead drifted off to a raw and unrefined world. Maybe that's why she turned to Mike.

Mike was a cop. He was my mother's boyfriend. He was not the first adulterous affair in my mother's life. I remember another cop, who was an earlier fling. But Mike proved to be a long-lasting relationship. He also became the manifestation of a shattered family, of preteen turmoil and of all that the recesses of my mind tried to repress for decades.

My mother was hardly secretive about the affair, at least with me. At times, she almost seemed to flaunt it. If Mike was scheduled to work the night shift, I would not be allowed to go upstairs when I came home from school for lunch. I was young and naive, but I wasn't stupid. I knew damn well who was upstairs. But what was I to do? So I would sit there alone, slowly chew my lunch, and then go back to school. Other times they were even more flagrant. His car would be parked in the drive-way, and when I would walk in the door Mike would be loung-ing in a comfortable chair downstairs. It got to a point where he became a fixture in our house, a constant reminder of a mother's callousness and a father's powerlessness.

Worse still, often I was used as a cover for them to see each other. Mike lived in Laurelton, a few stops farther on the

Long Island Railroad. Occasionally, while everyone was home during the evening, my mother would call to me: "I have to pick up some milk. Want to come along?" Somehow, I felt I had no choice. Although I was a headstrong kid, I could not say no to my mother. Maybe I was prodded by curiosity, but I became the foil so that she could get out of our house. What husband would suspect a wife of taking a daughter along while meeting a boyfriend? What mother could possibly so disregard a child's feelings? We would pick up Mike at the railroad station and drive him to his house, where Mom would kiss him or hug him and drop him off. When we returned home, I would go directly to my room. I couldn't bear to look at either of my parents. I felt so ashamed, as if I were guilty of something beyond my capacity to understand.

Eventually, I evolved from a co-conspirator to a victim. From time to time, when just the three of us rode in our two passenger Cadillac, my mother would drive while Mike and I shared the passenger seat next to her. I was twelve years old and just beginning to mature physically. One day, while I was sitting on his lap, he fondled me—right there in the passenger seat, and right next to my mother. When the trip ended, I ran from the car, my face flushed and my mind racing. I hated myself for being a coward, for not screaming or fighting him off. After that, whenever we were in the car together, he did it again. He did as he pleased. Later, he went even further.

There was a place called the Woodmere Docks, where young people would go to make out. Under the guise of teaching me how to drive, Mike took me there, and the groping began. At the time, I had difficulty discerning my feelings. Anger, excitement, nervousness, confusion. Perhaps because my mother's relationship with Mike made me so mad, so embarrassed, when he made overtures to me I may have felt as though I was getting back at her.

To have such a traumatic experience with an older man was both terrifying and titillating. I was a participant, and I didn't know whether I wanted it or didn't. I had always been an explorer, the kind of kid who wanted to know everything, do everything, participate in everything. An innate inquisitiveness—about relationships, about love, about people—led me to ask questions. I was curious about everything, including sexual experiences. I wanted to know what it was like. But when it happened to me, it was as if my mind was separated from my body. For the most part, I didn't want to think about it. Today, they call it child molestation. And I did feel like a victim, like somehow I had to do what he demanded. He was a policeman, an older man, a friend of my mother; I was a preteen being led toward taboo territory. Layers upon layers of authority hastened my acquiescence. We stopped just short of sex, but really it was the beginning of sex for me.

$\mathcal{B}$oys seemed to have a certain way of talking, certain rituals they followed, almost as if they were allowed to be spontaneous but knew that certain behaviors bolstered their boyishness. I would watch and listen, remaining intrigued into adolescence and adulthood. One of the ways of understanding, of course, is to have a sexual relationship. I liked to think that it wasn't a matter of being promiscuous as much as simply wanting to understand what made them tick.

I started high school at a young age. I wasn't quite thirteen when I began my four years at Woodmere High. I still loved the activity and companionship of boys, which eventually evolved into relationships with young men. I dated a basketball player for a while. He gave me a big "W" patch, and I sewed it on my sweater. Soon after, there was another boy, the son of a Middle Eastern shoe salesman. And then Morty came along.

Morty was a middle-class Jewish kid. He had a girlfriend named Leona who wasn't particularly attractive, but she had big breasts, and she set few limits as far as sex was concerned. One time I became, in a manner of speaking, a participant, too. Morty said to me, "You've got to come to Leona's house. She and I are going to make out. You just sit there." Amazingly, that's what I did. I sat there. They both knew I was there, but that didn't inhibit them. In fact, it seemed to make them both hungrier. And they had sex while I was in the room. It was dark, and I didn't see much of what went on. But I heard everything. It was another uncomfortable moment in my self-education.

Eventually, I lost my virginity to Morty. I viewed it as doing what I already had done, only more so. I found it exhilarating, part of the excitement arising from its taboo nature. We would find ways and places—in the house when nobody was home, in the car. It was frightening, too. We didn't use any form of birth control other than the notoriously unreliable withdrawal method, and I was always worrying about becoming pregnant. Right up until the time I became pregnant.

When I first found out, I was terrified. It was 1932. I was only sixteen, and it was just so wrong—the time in my life, the relationship, the shame it would bring upon my family. I had to do something, and Morty agreed. To his credit, I suppose, he didn't abandon me. He found a doctor in New York City who performed illegal abortions. Morty and I drove into the city, and I never actually saw the doctor. That is, I was blindfolded during the procedure. And I wasn't administered any sort of anesthesia. As barbaric as it sounds, I would characterize it simply as a very uncomfortable experience. Physically, it was painful, sort of like a bad period (and I certainly knew what that was like). But psychologically, my primary emotion was not guilt, but rather a sense of relief. Frankly, when I thought about it later, which wasn't often, I had no remorse. When women are forced to bring an unwanted child into the world, that child rarely ends up being happy. And at the time I was still a child myself.

Perhaps a year or so later, I broke up with Morty. After a while, he had become incredibly demanding. His uncle was in the jewelry business, so he would give me all sorts of necklaces and earrings. But he also took a good deal of self-esteem from me. He didn't want me to look at anybody else, and he had moments of violent behavior, so I was afraid of him. I don't think he ever struck me, but he threatened me constantly. I couldn't tolerate it anymore. Finally, I managed to break off the relationship. It was another reason why I never regretted my blindfolded minutes in the doctor's office.

Carolyn, age 16

After that, I went out with a number of people in high school. Their names and faces receded in my memory, but I recall one vivid moment when I returned home late one night after spending time with one of the young men. My mother was waiting for me. "Where were you? What were you doing?" I had long hair at the time, and she grabbed a clump of it and slapped me. "Don't you ever stay out late like that again." And this from a woman who was not exactly a model of chastity. But perhaps she was beginning to sense that I was emulating her. And maybe it bothered her. When I reflected on it later, it certainly bothered me.

My therapist used to describe me as a mixture of Athena (the intellect) and Penelope (the physical and emotional being). I think there were, indeed, two parts to me, and one often took precedence over the other. Sometimes I was the thinking person, and sometimes I was the woman who was all body, all physicality. But I admit that even during my marriage—despite having such a wonderful, adoring, and inspiring husband—I still found myself falling into the company of men. Forever after I tried to understand why I did it when I had one of the greatest guys in the world, why I often found myself drawn to men who had other women in their lives. I suppose the traumas of my childhood may have been a factor in my decisions—the fact that I often found comfort in companionship. For many years, I used to define myself through my relationship with others. It was my way of getting to know the world. But that may be a rationalization spawned by regret.

What I do know is this: To the extent that I was like my mother, I hated myself.

DISTANCE

*I*n the summers it remained light until 9 p.m., but when my mother's gold clock struck seven, it was time for me to go to bed. God, how I despised that gold clock. My mother would call for me outside, and I would pretend not to hear her. Often, my next-door neighbor Doris and I would hide in her father's truck. He was in the dry cleaning business, and when you closed the doors in the back of the truck, it was so dark that you could lose yourself in there—as black as midnight. In our fantasy, we were in command; we made the rules. I imagined that a mother's voice couldn't possibly penetrate the protective steel of a dry cleaner's fortress.

But then it would. Sissy was my family's pet name for me. "Time for bed, Sissy."

Doris would be allowed to stay up. I could hear the other kids playing outside. And I recalled a Robert Louis Stevenson poem that had seemed so appropriate to me:

In winter I get up at night
And dress by yellow candlelight
In summer quite the other way
I have to go to bed by day.
I have to go to bed to see
The birds still hopping on the tree
And hear the sounds of people's feet
Going past me in the street.

As a child, I'm sure the simple lack of freedom angered me, my not getting the kind of free rein my peers enjoyed. But perhaps a part of me, the maturing, reasoning soul in me, realized that my mother had a reason for tucking me away so early every evening. Less a matter of safety for her children, it was more that she didn't want to have to think about us, about where we were and what we were doing. When the gold clock struck seven, she could rid herself of that responsibility, if only for an evening. I learned later through my experience as a therapist and through therapy of my own that a child understands more than most adults believe possible. I began to perceive my mother's distance and to understand it more profoundly.

I realized it wasn't a matter of time at all; it was a matter of space.

The relationship between mother and child became the fulcrum of my life. As a daughter, it was a source of confusion and disappointment. As a mother, the relationships with my children provided me with my most profound joys and sorrow. Even outside the home later as a professional, parent–child relationships remained the focal point of my efforts. I inaugurated a program based on the belief that nurturing must be experienced before it can be expressed, that the cycle of mothering behavior is powerful and pervasive, and that trust is the basis for such a relationship. In some respects, my work evolved out of the cautionary tale of my mother and me.

Whatever my mother wanted as a child, she almost always received. Her parents had so much money and nobody else to lavish it on, a scenario that continued well into her marriage to my father. Indeed, it may have contributed to my father's lack of self-worth. My mother's father bought the house we moved into when I was nine, just over the Nassau County line in the town of Woodmere on the south shore of Long Island. There were five of us then—my mother my father, me, and a younger sister and brother, born after Eddie died. It was a beautiful house—brand new, brick, columned. In my childhood naivete, I saw photographs of Jefferson's Monticello and thought that our house was a version of that great mansion. My grandfather also bought

two Cadillacs, both for my mother, the driver in our family. My
father never drove. We lived about a block from the Long Island
Railroad, and he took the train into the city.

I, too, was a sometime beneficiary of my grandfather's gen-
erosity. He used to visit us in Woodmere. He was always very
snappy-looking—a straw hat, spats, a cane—and he would
always give me five dollars, which was quite a bit of money in
those days. He never carried anything except brand new bills. I
can only surmise that he must have gone to the bank every

Carolyn (left) and her grandfather
for a time, 1925

single day. But soon the five-dollar bills stopped coming because
Grandpa stopped visiting. He and my mother had fought bit-
terly, over what I was never sure, and he completely cut off relations with his daughter and her family. I later came to understand that the demise of their relationship was evidence of the
kind of upbringing my mother must have experienced. She had

had everything she wanted in the way of material things, but she may have lacked unconditional love and affection. That she later fell out of my life the way her father fell out of hers shows how powerful the cycle can be.

I don't think I ever saw my grandfather again. Another loss, another tragedy no one spoke of. Unspoken, too, was the dysfunctional relationship between my father and mother, between my mother and Mike, and between Mike and me. My mother must have known what Mike was doing to me. She must have. And I don't think I ever truly worked through my anger at her—for what happened to my father, for what happened to me, for all the things she wasn't.

I suspected that my father knew about the other men. He probably didn't know about Mike and me. I have no idea how he would have reacted. In no way violent, he was soft, gentle, a man who loved the outdoors and tended his garden with loving care, enjoying the work and the beauty. He was an intellectual, a voracious reader, and we had that in common. My father's genes allowed me to become immersed in a book in my bedroom, which was wallpapered with Dickens characters. Indeed, if this father and daughter shared anything it was *Great Expectations*—great, unmet expectations regarding Ruth Drucker.

I cringed at the way she spoke to him, demeaning him whenever she could. Perhaps worse, I grew to hate the silences, the separation. The routine was consistent at night, when sound often carries the farthest, and the quiet was deafening. I was sent to bed. I kissed my father goodnight as he sat in the den, his head buried in *The New York Times.* I reluctantly plodded to my room and sat there listening, the door cracked open slightly. Rarely did I hear any conversation. No talk about the day at work or the kids at school or anything that sounded like a desire to share . . . *something.* Instead, often only moments after I reached my room, I heard a light creak on the stairway. And then another and another. Always the sound of one pair of footsteps. No "Goodnight," only my mother creaking her way to her bedroom and shutting the door I imagined my father in his chair, still gripping the newspaper stealing glances toward the stairway as she climbed out of sight, then sighing and turning a page.

He loved her, I believe. He was attracted to her outgoing personality and her intelligence. But I can only conclude that she didn't love him. I don't know if she loved anybody. She didn't seem to care in the least about leaving him without a companion. I think she just felt she'd had enough of him, or that she needed more than he could give her. She wasn't necessarily malicious; she was simply self-centered. She did what she wanted to do, and sometimes her husband, her family, simply got in the way.

So my father probably knew about Mike, a betrayal that— like everything else in that house—remained unspoken. In retrospect I realize I lost respect for him because he did nothing about this state of affairs. It hurt me to feel that way, and perhaps he sensed it and was hurt by it, too. My husband, Bobby, also a nonviolent man once said, "There are only two things in life I would fight for—my woman and my politics." I don't know if my father felt the same about either one.

$\mathcal{I}$ believe another of my mother's behaviors led my father to finally give up: she had almost no limits to her spending. My father, a corporate lawyer, could not provide for her the way her wealthy parents had, but he made an adequate living. He could have supported a family comfortably if he had had a wife who would understand when he said, "Look, we have to go easy for a while. Times are tough. Money is tight." But my father could not say that, and my mother wasn't the type to listen.

She had no self-control. If something caught her eye, she bought it. At an elegant shoe store on Madison Avenue called J&J Slater she would pay fifty dollars for shoes, maybe more—a tremendous amount of money back then. The shoes were gorgeous, but I don't know if she even wore them. She seemed to buy them just to have them. She hardly ever got dressed up. The only time I ever saw her beautifully attired was in old photos, snapshots from their wedding. Yet she ran up bills she couldn't pay.

In 1928, these debts forced us to leave our lovely home in Woodmere and move to a smaller house in a lower middle-class neighborhood on the other side of town. Many changes arrived in our life. No more housekeepers for the Drucker family. No more handouts from her father. In fact, her profligate ways may have been what drove a wedge between my mother and my grandfather. He knew she was spending more than she had, and after a while he was no longer willing to pay her debts.

When she wasn't buying, she was giving money away—to Mike. Not only the money my father made and the money her father gave her, but money that I received from my grandfather, too. I used to save nearly every crisp five-dollar bill. Over the years, I saved quite a bit. But one day my mother told me Mike needed money for something, and I gave it to her.

She insisted that Mike would repay it, going so far as to make it formal. We sat down at the kitchen table, and she scribbled a few promises on a piece of paper—a "sum received" and an "interest thereon from this date at the rate of . . .." Then she signed it with a flourish, smiling as if it were natural for a mother to borrow money from her daughter to fund her lover's needs. I kept the note in my room, but before it was repaid, she again took money from me for Mike. Once more, she wrote up a promissory note, and again I believed her that the money would be repaid. I don't know how many times it happened, but I believed her every time. She was an adult. She was my mother. I kept those promissory notes for several years—kept them until I realized they were worthless.

My grandparents had given my mother the most magnificent silverware and serving dishes, enough to fill a large cabinet. But she sold it all for cash, much of it going to Mike. She had exquisite jewelry, too. I remember a pin shaped like a tree branch, and from this branch were smaller branches, each bearing a different precious gem at the end—ruby, diamond, emerald, sapphire. She sold that, too. The watch of blue enamel with a little diamond in the back that hung from a platinum chain? Sold. We had a grand old house full of handcrafted furniture. Gone, all gone. Sometimes I think she made a concerted effort to rid herself of everything that might reflect her upper-class background. There was no rhyme or reason to it. She was a rebel without a cause.

In the end, she was a rebel who had alienated her entire family. Her father had disowned her. Her husband had chosen a different escape. Her first son was dead. Her second son had all but disappeared. Her daughters had little to do with her. By the time I was married and living on Manhattan's Upper West Side, she was a distant remnant of my past, more ghost than mother. I saw her less and less frequently after my wedding, until it soon became not at all. I just had no need for her in my life and didn't find any pleasure in being with her at all. It probably says a lot about her and a lot about me.

Then one day in 1955 the doorbell rang in my apartment, and there she was, carrying one tiny suitcase. It held everything she had left in the world. It was as if a stranger were standing there. She was only sixty-five then, not very old, but the years lay heavily upon her. Until then, the last I heard of her, she had been working as a housekeeper and companion to an elderly lady. She didn't look well, and I sent her to my doctor, who admitted her to Mt. Sinai Hospital. I didn't think she was all that sick, but the end came quickly. Ruth Drucker had lost her will to live. Her world had crumbled—and she with it.

My mother had always been an independent woman, per- haps too much so. By that I mean she had separated herself even from those to whom she might have been closest. When she finally realized she needed me, she came to me. But not until the end of her life.

What so saddened me about our disintegrated relationship was the consideration of what might have been. We had several decades over which we could have established perhaps the most profound bond two people can share. And it was wasted. What imprint did she leave on my subconscious? I'm not sure. But my conscious images of her consisted primarily of fading recollections, harsh judgments, disappointments, and lessons in what not to do. Even my anger at her seemed to fade over the years. I was left with few lasting impressions.

Sometimes I wondered whether I could have reached out to her more, expressed my feelings, misgivings, resentments, and desires. Then I reminded myself: It takes one hand to reach out and another to take it.

MELODIES UNHEARD

I've left the figures, the threat of them,

The numbers we add to measure hope

Or promise or peace. And an ancient song

Tuned to an archaic key

Played on a modern flute

Had buried its sound in me.

Is it old music—like a marching song

A commanding melody that climbs the hills,

Like a flooding river on a mighty run?

Or is it old music—like a sighing thing,

Like a sifted leaf in the winnowing wind,

Or the echo of an unanswered call?

Or is there no tone at all

But the sound of the rushing surf

The slush of a rowboat in the sand

The glimpse of the mirror in the moon

Sending no voice from the sun's days

But a gleam of sight to the tilt of time?

Pipe to me ditties of no tone, he said,

And fix the passion, fan the fire,

With melodies unheard—that ancient song—perhaps

On a silent flute in a modern key.

—Bobby Goodman

THE POET AND THE SWORD

$\mathcal{W}$hen I graduated from high school in 1932, my parents couldn't really afford to send me to college. However, New York University's tuition was somewhat reasonable at the time, so I spent two years studying there, all the while dreaming of leaving home. Then I found out there was a state-funded School of Home Economics (now called the College of Human Ecology) at Cornell University in Ithaca, New York. There was no tuition. You just had to pay for your room and board. My parents agreed that they could manage those expenses, so off I went.

I never found the academics particularly challenging at Cornell. I did all right—not remarkable, but fine. Although I majored in home economics, and although I found it enjoyable and figured it was where I was probably going to make a living, a big part of me wanted to escape notions of domesticity. After all, I was finally away from home for the first time. So I took as many courses as possible in the liberal arts. I wanted to be a bit less practical, a tad more intellectual.

My biggest weakness was math, and for this I can blame my mother as well as myself. As a child, I would bring my arithmetic homework home and leave it on the table. The next morning, I would wake up, and the work would be done. My mother did it. She never said anything (everything seemed to be unsaid in that house), and I would just take it to school. But as I got older and moved into algebra and higher math, I found myself lacking the necessary knowledge. Over the years, I never got any better at math, having to add columns several times before I found the right answer. It's funny, I suppose, that I would marry an engineer. But really, he was a man of words, not numbers.

I reveled in my freedom as a college student. I joined the Alpha Epsilon Phi sorority and met a lot of young men. Many of them took me out to dinner, which was a good thing because I couldn't afford to eat out on my own. A fellow named Ralph, a handsome man who was studying to become a doctor, was one of the men who asked me out, and along the way he introduced me to his roommate, Bobby Goodman, who was dating another young woman at the time. When Bobby and I met, I felt a certain attraction, an almost intuitive feeling that we had much in

common. He seemed like a poet, a dreamer, a wonderful innocent. In some ways, he reminded me of my father.

Bobby had full, black hair and dark brown eyes. He certainly wasn't a typical college man in how he dressed and what
his interests were. He wore baggy clothes, and I always saw him
in the same tweed suit, which looked like he must have owned it
forever. I would see him here and there, and I would hear people
talk about him. Eventually, I found myself maneuvering to be in
the same place as he, often at the campus bookstore.

Then came Junior Week, a time when all the men were
expected to move out of their fraternity houses and their dates
for that weekend were to move in. The men didn't move out, of
course, and the so-called chaperones were not much older than
we were. It was one of those romance-in-the-air weekends, but
Bobby, who had broken up with his girlfriend, didn't have a date.

My date was Ralph, and I found him dull as dishwater. So
I began talking to Bobby, who was wandering aimlessly around
the festivities. The more I talked to Bobby, the less I talked to
Ralph. The less attention I paid to Ralph, the more he drank.
Eventually, Ralph passed out. There I was, and there Bobby was,
and he said, "Look, you can come up and sleep in my room if you
want to." And then he did the cutest thing. He set a mattress on
the floor, pulled out a long sword he had picked up during one
of his many travels as a boy, and placed it in the middle of the
mattress. "You sleep on this side," he said. "I'll sleep on the other

side." As it turned out, the sword didn't stay there too long. From that very first night, we knew we were perfect for each other.

The other young men had called me beautiful and talked of love, but it only *sounded* like love—it didn't feel like it. They fed my ego but not my soul. While they figuratively offered me a mirror when speaking of beauty, Bobby offered me a poem or a painting or a song whose beauty belonged to music, art, and nature. His gifts were wrapped in an eagerness to share the experience with me. Without his having to declare it, I knew he loved me as much as I cherished him.

Carolyn, age 21

With Bobby, love was . . . unadorned. There was no pretense, no phoniness. Whatever he knew, in the way of the beautiful things in life, he wanted to share. His mother had died only a year earlier, and it had devastated him. But in the Goodman house, unlike the Drucker house, if you had something to say, you said it. So Bobby wrote a letter to his dying mother upon arriving for his first autumn in Ithaca:

Dear Mother,

We drove to school, and the drive was pleasant, merely that and nothing more. Let your mind wander, if you will, to any day of sunshine, to any day of joy and happiness, and picture four boys together in a car on their way to school. When the picture comes before you, smile at the ease with which they talk, laugh at the things which amuse them; then close your eyes and rest your head, and say that there is something good in the world, something which, if you will it, is yours to have and yours to remember.

Suppose I make a demand of you and say in rather absolute terms that I want you to live my experiences from day to day; suppose you think as I do, react as I do to people and events about me; suppose you go to college with me, study with me, develop an interest in the outside world of commonplace events, laugh at the follies of man, overlook their faults, and love humanity on a grand scale, a scale so large that it covers the world. Let us, together, create for ourselves a huge bubble that can never burst, and let us make this bubble a transparent container of our actions, but never let me call them our illusions, never let me pierce the thin covering that encloses our troubles and our joys.

But there is one thing I demand (if a son may demand anything of a mother), and the demand is simple, and must be obeyed. You must smile when I smile, and if ever a note of gloom enters upon my consciousness, you must smile at me; in fact, you must laugh at me and say, "The impetuous youth is afflicted with the common disease of serious neophytes, and is now a bit moody. I remember, only too well, those ambitious ideals that were going to set the world on fire, and now I have a son who seems to wish to continue where I more or less became a bit practical and hitched my wagon to home instead of a star."

This must be our pact; this must be our guide; this must always be the string which binds the opening in our bubble; this must help us realize, in spite of pain and trouble, that heaven is one large circle, and its center is everywhere. A bit idealistic, I must confess, but nevertheless it must be true; and, what is a great deal more important, you must believe it, and smile when you can. Thus you will bring light to your world and to many others that are linked with and depend on yours for their brightness.

It is difficult for me to begin. I am happy, and you lie in bed. But you must never think of the contrast. You must understand that by the rules of our agreement, you are living in Ithaca and living with me. When I act, you act, and New York is no more, and beds are places where people sleep at night, merely that and nothing more— if you will it, and I know you can.

R-E-M-E-M-B-E-R   O-U-R   B-U-B-B-L-E

Love, Bob

Typical, beautiful Bobby. The contrast, of course, between my experiences and his relationship with the woman who gave him life was startling. His was a magical dance between mother and son, cut painfully short yet so much more powerful and enduring. I never knew Rose Goodman. I only knew her through Bobby's eyes, through his stories of her beauty and talent. She was a Polish immigrant, a proud socialist, a poet, a pianist. And Bobby was his mother's son. You could see it in his politics, his love of music, his ability to turn a blank page into a kaleidoscope of color and emotion. Rose Goodman played a seminal role in her son's development—even while she was dying at the age of forty-three, ravaged by cancer as her oldest son took leave of her for the last time and headed to the halls of higher learning. And even then she lived on.

Bobby would read poetry to me for hours—Browning, Shelley, Byron, or Keats's "Ode to a Grecian Urn." He would bolster the words with fascinating background, explaining to me, for instance, how Byron fought in the wars for freedom in Greece. He was always sharing gems like that. Those were the gifts he gave me.

We both graduated in 1936, Bobby with a bachelor's degree in English literature. But he returned to Cornell the following year in a fifth-year program to earn a degree in civil engineering. His father, himself a civil engineering graduate from Cooper Union, had put tremendous pressure on Bobby to follow in his footsteps so he could "get a good job." Bobby would not let him down.

But he remained an artist and poet at heart. An artist-engineer may seem like a contradiction, but I think they were merely the components that made up my husband's yearning to create and construct, to make sense of the world. He saw beauty and grandeur in the works of great builders of roads, dams, and bridges. "You can reach the stars better by setting rivets sometimes," he once explained, "than by lapsing into ecstasies over the moon."

Whatever project he was working on was nothing less than a poem to him. I will never forget the first time we glimpsed the completed George Washington Bridge. It was lit up beautifully at night, and Bobby took me to see it. "Look at that, darling," he said, putting his arm around me. "A string of pearls across the Hudson River."

He could make magic from the most mundane. I vividly recall our walks up and down the hills of Ithaca. On one of these walks, he pulled out a potato chip, held it up, stared at it. "Do you know," he asked, turning to me, "what goes into making this potato chip?" Then he talked about the farmer, the manufacturer, the distributor, how much money was made, and how the hard-working farmers often received little for their labor. He was laying out the capitalist system, explaining the possibilities for exploitation and the potential for change. How many people could explain this complicated system and make it fascinating to a young woman who then listened with rapt attention? He was a theoretician, a philosopher. But that was also the poet in him, the artist. How many men could paint the world on a potato chip?

Still, Bobby was mortal. In that fifth year at Cornell he suddenly didn't feel right, so he went to the medical clinic for a check-up. He thought maybe he had a lingering cold, or perhaps he had just overtaxed himself and was suffering from exhaustion. But the doctors came back with a diagnosis—tuberculosis.

Needless to say, it was a devastating revelation. How he contracted it, we were never sure. It might have been going around his Alpha Epsilon Pi fraternity house. (The fact that he was even in a fraternity is rather strange because he simply wasn't the type, although it is noteworthy that a quarter century later Mickey Schwerner was in the same fraternity at Cornell.) Somehow, Bobby had joined the many sufferers of an epidemic that was blazing through the western world killing tens of thousands of people annually; indeed, TB may have caused the largest number of deaths in history, perhaps a billion people in the last two centuries alone. Tragically, TB often strikes young people in the prime of their lives, people like my beloved Bobby. The Greek historian Herodotus, someone to whom Bobby might have felt a particular kinship, once poignantly stated that "in the time of plague it is the parents who bury their children." The reality of that, of course, would hit home for Bobby and me nearly three decades later—the plague this time not a disease but a cycle of hatred and violence.

Tuberculosis also carried with it a stigma at the time, not entirely unlike that associated with the modern HIV virus, even after the patients had been successfully treated. Employers were reluctant to hire disease carriers. People were reluctant to marry them—women because TB might diminish their husbands' earning potential, and men because it might prevent their wives from bearing children. Even health care workers were frightened of the highly contagious disease, which was considered such an occupational hazard that a great many of the physicians and employees of tuberculosis sanatoriums had already been treated for the disease themselves. One of the first questions health care personnel were asked upon arriving was, "Where were you cured?"

Naturally, all of us who loved Bobby were frightened, too. Clearly, he would have to devote himself fully to recovery, so he went home to New York City. But his parents immediately sent him away to the Trudeau Sanatorium (as it was then called) in Saranac Lake, New York, in the foothills of the Adirondack Mountains. There was a hospital on the grounds, but recovering patients were housed in cottages, each furnished with a hospital bed that could be wheeled through French doors onto a screened porch. Its library held an extensive collection of fiction and nonfiction, including the works of Robert Louis Stevenson, who had been a patient there himself a half century earlier. The author Walker Percy would recover there some five years later. At least Bobby was in good company.

What the library didn't have was some of the leftist books that Bobby desired. So he asked his father, Charles, to locate the three volumes of Marx's *Das Kapital* and all of Lenin's works. Now, Charles and Bobby never really saw eye-to-eye politically. They could get into some remarkably heated arguments. But Charles adored his oldest child, and he brought him those books. Politics were one thing; family was quite another.

Still, Bobby suffered. With the discovery of streptomycin just a few years away, he was forced to undergo a periodic procedure known as artificial pneumothorax, which produced temporary collapse of the infected lung, putting it "at rest" and allowing the tubercular cavities to heal. But the primary

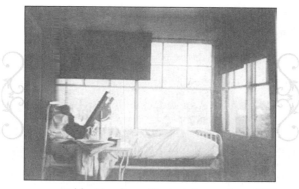

Bobby Goodman, Trudeau Sanatorium, 1937

treatment was complete bed rest, virtually nothing else. Bobby couldn't stand it.

My grandfather had left me enough money to afford a car, so on my days off I would drive up to the sanatorium and visit him. I could see why Bobby desperately wanted to leave. A pleasant enough camp-like atmosphere made it certainly far better than the hundreds of inner-city sanatoriums around the country, but my primary recollection of the place revolved around the incessant coughing . . . and coughing . . . and coughing. Not knowing how long he would be kept there, Bobby made a decision: One night, he simply packed his bags, boarded a train, and came home.

His family was obviously a little shocked to see him, but they were also relieved. They didn't want him to be that far away either. So they purchased a "cure chair"—a full-length lounge with an adjustable back so that he could sit up or recline. And they set him up with an apartment in the building that Charles Goodman's company had built—the El Dorado on Ninetieth Street and Central Park West. His place was higher than the thirtieth floor, way up in the tower, and he stayed there until the family made plans to visit their summer home at Tupper Lake, which was back in the Adirondacks. Charles Goodman provided a place for his son there, a little house outside the main house.

Really, the goal of Bobby's treatment was to get him a healthy dose of fresh air. But Bobby took it too far sometimes.

He would get out on the tennis court and start hitting the ball around. It drove me crazy!

"Bobby, for God's sake, give it more time!" I implored him. But he didn't want to be a patient in any sense of the word. He wanted to be free—free of the disease, free to wander as he might.

I imagine freedom as a theme running through my life and the lives of the many people who contributed to the pieces of me. My ancestors wanted to be free from religious persecution, so they traveled across an ocean in search of a place to feel at home. My mother wanted to spend freely, love freely, perhaps be free of family obligation. My middle son traveled to Mississippi to free southern African-Americans from the fear and discrimination that prevented political and cultural freedom. He gave his life for it.

If I could pick a moment that encapsulates all of that, however, my mind conjures up an autumn image of Bobby. I had visited him at the sanatorium, and for the first time since he arrived at Trudeau I was able to take him into the real outdoors, not just a screened-in porch. We wandered into the woods, where the forest floor was covered with gorgeous fallen leaves of every color. Bobby climbed out of the car, ran beneath the trees, and threw himself on the ground, kissing the earth.

It was a moment that stayed with me always: Freedom.

ONE ARM OVER THE OTHER

$\mathcal{E}$arly autumn of 1938 may have been the most untroubled time of my life. Bobby had asked me to marry him. We scheduled an October wedding, and only two weeks before the big day we were spending some time at his parents' summer home in Tupper Lake. Late September in the Adirondacks is when the foliage is in full frenzy. The air shifts, and the leaves suddenly burst into countless shades of red, orange, and yellow. The explosion of color that adorned the mountains and lakeshores mirrored my hopefulness. There was, indeed, something in the air, crisply defined—a new beginning.

It had been nearly two decades since my brother had disappeared from my life in a single evening. For a while after that, I had suffered a dread of random tragedy—the fear that my world could be spinning along comfortably until an unforeseen shock caused it to wobble, when suddenly my life would career out of control. Over the years, however, the apprehension had ebbed until it had been replaced by optimism. Bobby had recovered. We were about to become life partners. The leafy trees were revealing infinite possibilities.

Then the phone rang at the house in Tupper Lake.

As my mother gradually had become more and more distant, and as her behavior was increasingly devoid of compassion, I had begun to grow closer to my father. He was a dreamer, a man who loved nature, a man of intellect. He would occasionally set off for the Adirondacks himself, where he would climb some of the highest peaks to enjoy the surrounding beauty. Tragically, his life became an insurmountable mountain. The harder he climbed, the more unattainable the peak seemed to be.

Edward Drucker commuted every day into Manhattan, working hard to raise a family, trying in vain to make enough money to satisfy his wife. Often, I visited him at work, and he and I roamed the city together. I got all dressed up in a beautiful gray coat and velvet hat that my grandfather had bought for me, took the Long Island Railroad into the city, and waited for him. Sometimes the wait seemed endless, and I spent the time gazing at the Hudson River from his offices in the Woolworth Building. I always felt as if I were on friendly terms with the Statue of

Liberty, who so often stared back at me from the bay. When my
father's work was done, we stopped at the Washington Market
and watched the grocer make peanut butter. We bought a carton
of it and maybe purchased some exotic cheeses. Or we walked
down Chamber Street, where Stump & Walter sold seeds and
plants. Dad would buy rose bushes and other assorted things of
beauty. He couldn't wait to get home to plant them. His garden
was his escape.

Gradually, we developed a close relationship, Dad and I. But
it wasn't until I was on the verge of marrying Bobby that my
father began to confide in me. One day, I drove with him to the
public beach in Woodmere. It was late in the summer, and the
beach was nearly empty. We sat there in the parking lot, and we

talked undisturbed for hours. He said he was depressed, that he felt as if he had no future. His law firm was not doing well, and his marriage was falling apart. He had nothing to look forward to. He was doing his best, but it wasn't enough for him.

I later realized that his greatest sadness at the time may have been related to my impending marriage. I was his one bulwark, always there for him. He was very fond of Bobby, but he may have felt that if he lost me he would have nothing left. I was his beloved daughter, and I was leaving the nest. Later, the guilt I felt was almost overwhelming. Why didn't I tell someone? Why didn't I get him some help, find a way to give him more support than I knew how to provide? My understanding of the depths of his depression had limitations. After all, I was twenty-two years old and in love. That dominated my life at the time. Maybe I expected my happiness to extend to my father. Maybe I expected too much.

A few weeks after that conversation at Woodmere beach I found myself at Tupper Lake answering the telephone. A voice on the other end told me the news: Daddy had killed himself, had shot himself in a hotel room.

All of that aggression that I wished he had shown over the years, all of that anger, had turned inward. Obviously, I was devastated. What do you do when your father, the person you believe you're supposed to rely on for strength and support, decides his life is futile? Should I have seen it coming? Could I have done more to alleviate his misery? I raced home. I wanted to be with him—too late.

I also wanted to put off our wedding, which I had expected to be the happiest day of my life. But I was talked out of doing so by a close friend of ours, a rabbi. In fact, I wanted him to ask God why on earth he would let such a thing happen. But God and I had a complicated relationship. When I was young, my girlfriends went to Sunday school, and upon deciding I wanted to be more like them, I did too. So I learned a bit about the foundations of religious tradition. But I didn't learn Hebrew, and we didn't celebrate Jewish holidays. We celebrated Christmas and not Hanukkah (though we did stay home from school on the Jewish High Holy Days; my father figured it was the right thing to do). I never recall feeling the sting of anti-Semitism. But then religion itself never had much of an impact on me.

Still, my friend the rabbi insisted. "Don't postpone the wedding," he said. "In Jewish law, you never put off your marriage date. You always go ahead with it." So we had a very simple wedding, just a few people and a small dinner. My mother was there.

We even managed to approximate a honeymoon, though that, too, didn't go in the direction we originally planned. Bobby and I loved mountain climbing, and we planned to visit the Blue Ridge Mountains. But for some reason the roads were terribly crowded as we headed south. We feared we were going to spend the first night of our honeymoon on the road, so we turned around. We actually spent that first night at the Essex House on Central Park South. The next day, we jointly decided to head north instead. Looking back, given what later happened to our son Andy in the Deep South, I recognize the irony of the choice. But we wound up going to Cape Cod, to Provincetown, and we spent our honeymoon there.

Bobby and Carolyn
on their wedding day

After that, we both went back to Cornell, so that Bobby could complete his engineering degree. He had only a few months to go. In those few months, Bobby essentially traded his liberal arts pursuits for the nuts and bolts of a more directly applicable education. Meanwhile, I basically did the opposite. I was aching to explore my artistic side, so I took courses in painting and sculpture and spent hours in the fine arts building. It was almost as if I were constructing a new person, a new life. An extended honeymoon, it was obviously a bittersweet experience, a profound transition really. My father's death still weighed heavily on me, despite my attempts at distraction— the artistic immersion, the strolls through the gorges and plantations at Cornell, even the nightly comfort of the arms of my new husband.

Subsequent experience has given me insight into what my father must have been going through toward the very end. He must have seen his life, his world, as one dark hole. At times, I certainly have felt the same way. When I hear of people mired in depression, I fear for them because I have known too much of it, both within myself and in some of the people to whom I have been closest. But I am always amazed at the inner resources we can summon in our darkest periods, and I summoned them when my father died.

I long ago discovered a secret to surviving, a method I used for more than three quarters of a century. I would just think back to the early 1920s and summers at Echo Lake.

I was eight when I first went to summer camp in Readfield, Maine, a small town in the state's Central Lakes region. When you first arrived at the camp, before you passed the swim test, you had to swim in an enclosed area. The Crib, we called it, and everybody wanted to escape the Crib as soon as possible. The counselors would observe you, and when they thought you were ready you would take the fateful test. During the Red Cap test (performed while wearing a red bathing cap), the counselors would get into a boat and row beside you as you swam out to a point and back. I had been raised near the beach, and I considered myself a pretty good swimmer, so I guess I volunteered a bit prematurely.

In light of the course of my life it seems strange to say this, but endurance was my problem. I simply did not have the capacity to swim long distances. But I knew if I failed to make it to that point and back, I would be in the Crib perhaps the whole summer, and I didn't want that. I started out okay, but on the way back from the point I began to huff and puff, struggling to keep afloat. The counselors could see it and hear it.

"C'mon, Carolyn," they said after a while. "Get in the boat. You can try again next week."

I kept going. I kept huffing. I kept puffing.

"Carolyn, c'mon. Get in the boat! Summer's just beginning. You can try it again in a few days."

But I was thinking, "Next week is not going to be any easier." So I said to myself, *Carolyn, just put one arm over the other. One arm over the other. Just keep going. And don't stop.*

And I made it. Barely, but I made it. Ever after, when I felt I was going under, when I suffered a loss so great that there appeared no chance of ever raising my head above water again,

I just kept telling myself over and over: *Carolyn, just keep going. One arm over the other, one over the other.*

TUPPER LAKE

There is sweetness here and the quiet love of internal peace

There is subtle joy and the warm comfort of tender thought

There is calm and sunshine and tenuous softness

And full measure of conjugal bliss.

There are young voices and glad tokens of playfulness

Sparkling water and rushing murmur at the shore

There are trees and wind—gentle wind and the hush of sifting waywardness

Soft winds—and the brush of the leaves, and the lilt of the woods.

There are clouds—and whiteness and the cool comfort of a blue sky

There's a bar of contentment in a sea of song.

—Bobby Goodman

A BAR OF CONTENTMENT
IN A SEA OF SONG

*B*obby was unabashedly passionate about music. He played the violin—not too well, really, but he played it. However, he was a world-class listener who, to my everlasting joy, would stand up and cheer madly at the end of a symphony. Over the years, we became active supporters of all the arts, but especially music, which emerged as an essential component of the Goodman household. Before unions represented performers in New York City, we arranged for musicians to perform chamber music in our large Eighty-sixth Street apartment. We invited dozens of guests at a time, requesting a cover charge and then giving the money to underpaid members of groups like the New York Philharmonic. Occasionally, too, musical icons like Leonard Bernstein could be found tickling the ivories of the Goodman family piano.

Bobby and I were among the early donors to the Lincoln Center for the Performing Arts, endowing a seat in the New York Philharmonic Hall. Later, I became a board member and fundraiser for Symphony Space on Broadway and Ninety-fifth Street, its stated mission being to foster artistically and culturally diverse performing arts, literary, and film programs. That happened purely by chance.

Walking up Broadway one morning, I spotted a prominent violinist ahead of me, walking in the same direction. *Where was he going?* Always curious, I decided to follow him. He walked into an abandoned movie house that had been recently renovated. The marquee read, "Wall-to-Wall Bach!" and the place was full of people. I sat there listening to wonderful performances all day—I mean, for hours and hours. I only took breaks to grab a sandwich or a snack. When I called their number the next day and asked exactly what was happening there, just like that I became a fundraiser for Symphony Space. My first effort involved raising $15,000 for the installation of acoustic panels in the building.

But for Bobby and me, music was more than another cultural outlet or social cause. It was sustenance. Music was a conduit to myriad emotions and, when necessary, an outlet for them, too. Generally, amid all the turmoil and tragedy of my life, through good times and bad, music provided a respite from the weight of the world.

The only other part of my life that could match the symphony as a consistently pleasurable escape was that place in the mountains, the house in Tupper Lake. In fact, that began as a musical story, too.

Charles Goodman, Bobby's father, was an outstanding engineer. He was involved in construction of the New York State Thruway, the Brooklyn Battery Tunnel, and the Eldorado Apartments. Indeed, he went completely broke while building and owning the latter in 1929, when he lost everything. But he made a brilliant comeback, even during the Depression, returning to build again. In 1934, he constructed an homage to his wife.

Charles was a very practical man who was married to a musically gifted woman with whom he was totally in love. Rose Goodman spent some of her happiest moments in Lake Placid with her music teacher, Clarence Adler, at what he called his summer music camp—everything out there was a camp; our house came to be known to the locals as the Goodman Camp. So Charles decided to build a house a day's drive from New York City in Tupper Lake, thirty miles west of Lake Placid.

When he drove up to scope out the area, he happened upon construction of a road connecting Long Lake with Tupper Lake, a distance of about twenty miles. The crews blasting through the mountains to build the road left enormous rocks lying all over the roadside. Charles, always creatively practical, asked the field engineer what he planned to do with all the rocks. The man told him, "We're going to have to get trucks and carry them away." Charles replied, "I'll do it for you." And he did. That's how he built the house at Tupper Lake—all out of the exquisite granite of the Adirondack Mountains.

Carolyn in front of Charles
Goodman's stone house

It was a magnificent house on a hill—nine bedrooms, nearly as many baths, a big living room, a basement with a pool table and ping-pong table, and a boathouse down the hill along the lakeshore, where Bobby and I and the kids would later stay. The house on the hill had a tremendous amount of bookshelves, but Charles didn't have nearly enough books to fill them. So he went to a secondhand bookshop on Third Avenue and bought a yard of Shakespeare, a yard of Dickens. He was the only man I ever knew who bought books by the yard.

Most houses in the Adirondacks were made of wood. So many trees and so few logging restrictions thus meant so many wooden buildings, from log cabins to beautiful structures like the Saranac Lake Inn. I remember visiting the Inn with the Goodman family and marveling at it. A long, one-story building, all white with a red roof, it had been built at the turn of the century with dozens of rooms. "This is magnificent," I said to no one in particular. "Look at this place. It's beautiful!"

And then Charles Goodman replied with two words that revealed so much—not only about him but also about the home he built out of the Adirondacks, a house that would endure as a monument to his beloved Rose and her family despite her dying before it was finished. Charles took a long look at the wooden Saranac Lake Inn and then turned to me, shaking his head and raising a single finger.

"One match . . ." he said.

Not only did one woman's passion for the piano lead to the creation of that wonderful mountain retreat, later generations took up the same passion. All our children gravitated to a musical instrument of one kind or another, each of them spending several years in the pre-college division of Juilliard.

After graduating from NYU, Jonny was accepted into the incredibly competitive Juilliard Graduate School of Music, training as a choral and orchestral conductor. Later (admittedly, to my disappointment) he traded in that opportunity for a life of piety as a Lubavitcher, a member of a Hasidic community. Still, people used to tell me he was an amazing piano player and one of the most talented musicians they had ever met. As his unbiased mother, I could only agree. Of course, he never had the inclination to truly capitalize on it. That's just the way he is. For him, it was music for music's sake, which—like faith, I suppose—is the purest form of all.

Andy, too, had a profound passion for music. Typical of his honesty with his emotions, at concerts he would be so moved that tears would flow. His father was exactly the same way. Andy played the clarinet, and he owned a pretty good one, sold to us by a teacher at Walden School. "Don't worry," the teacher told us, well aware that Andy was an active preteen boy. "This is unbreakable."

So one day Andy was practicing on that clarinet in his bedroom. My bedroom was next to his, and I was sitting in there, reading and listening. Soon I realized I hadn't heard anything for some time. And then, suddenly, I heard a crash . . . and silence. When I ran into the room, there stood Andy, with a rather stunned look on his face. He was holding only the stem of his unbreakable clarinet. The horn part was in pieces on the floor.

"Andy, what on earth happened?" I asked.

"Mom, I don't really know," he said. "I was practicing, and all of a sudden I thought of Jackie Robinson up at bat. And a fastball was coming. And I swung at it."

So that was the story of the unbreakable clarinet. But to my great pleasure, I was still able to hear that beautiful sound long after. Andy's younger brother, David, played the oboe very well. And David's oldest son, Jacob, also became an excellent musician. He chose the clarinet, just like the uncle he never knew. And when he played it at his eighth grade graduation, so beautifully and with such feeling, I began to cry. Because I could swear that was Andy playing that clarinet.

Music always meant more to me than mere sound. It was the experience, the emotion, the way a melody could unite or uplift or galvanize or encapsulate a weighty memory. For that reason I insisted that song be an integral part of my memorial service after I was gone. Yes, I was significantly involved in planning it. Who wouldn't want to plan their grand exit? Besides, nobody who knew me well would expect anything otherwise. So I compiled a list of possible speakers at the service, and I imagined a series of remembrances interspersed with profound melodies.

The service would begin with the sounding of the shofar, a hauntingly beautiful instrument made from the horn of a ram that has signified many different elements of Jewish identity over the epochs—from liberty to solidarity to renewal.

Moments later, a lovely contralto singer with a powerful voice would belt out "Amazing Grace." The lyrics would seem like a narration of my journey:

Through many dangers, toils, and snares
I have already come;
'Tis Grace that brought me safe thus far
And Grace will lead me home.

Doug Mishkin, a lawyer from Washington, D.C., and a noted singer/songwriter whom I got to know quite well over the years (along with his brother, Budd), would play the guitar and sing Peter, Paul, and Mary's "Sweet Survivor," one of my favorite songs. The remarkable Harry Belafonte would be there, too, offering his version of "Those Three Are on My Mind," Pete Seeger's heart-wrenching song about the Mississippi horror, its lyrics lamenting "Andy in the cold wet clay." Finally, several members of an African-American choir from a local church would take the stage. During the darkest and most intense times of the civil rights struggle, music from that era was perhaps as responsible as anything for galvanizing the spirit and the collective will of the movement. So I requested a series of gospel and freedom songs, including "We Shall Overcome":

We shall overcome, we shall overcome,
We shall overcome some day
Oh, deep in my heart, I do believe
We shall overcome some day

I could envision the service coming to a close with a jazz
trumpeter and that magical choir belting out "When the Saints
Go Marching In" and then heading for the doors, leaving the
notes and notions of that sanguine song to echo in the rafters
and in the hearts of my loved ones:

We are trav'ling in the footsteps
Of those who've gone before
And we'll all be reunited,
On a new and sunlit shore . . .

THE ZEST OF THEIR
LEAPING EYES

$\mathcal{O}$n a warm afternoon when I was in my early eighties, I was staring at the sun-swept waters of Mill Pond alongside the small house I rented in the Hamptons each summer. Suddenly, a family of swans glided by, floating into view in a space between the thickets of grass. There were two adult swans and three young ones. It was August, the time of year when they're old enough to move around in their milieu. These little swans were probably a month old and were now ready to swim.

The mother was in front, and she turned her long, beautiful neck around to look at her babies, to make sure they were right in back of her, staying the course. The father was in back, also watching intently, ensuring that the little ones were doing what they were taught to do, going where they were supposed to go.

Later, when the swans are older, they will surely veer off in different directions, exploring the farthest reaches of the pond, swimming away at odd angles toward unknown parts. But for now, the three young ones were all in a line between their guardians, following in the wake of their mother looking back, protected by their father looking forward.

It struck me that no matter how much you think you may be keeping your children in line, no matter how much it seems that they are all being shepherded on a particular course or brought up in a similar environment, they are eventually going to find their own way. They're going to head off in their own direction, according to what their own hearts tell them to do. Nature diversifies, and time disperses. It is the way of things, and it always will be. And I came to revel in that aspect of my children, if not my own siblings.

Family dynamics always fascinated me. The difference between my two immediate families—the one in which I was raised and the one in which I raised my children—is remarkable. In my later work in clinical psychology, I spoke often of breaking cycles, stopping unhealthy behaviors from repeating in the next generation. I like to think that I did that as a parent.

After the death of my older brother, Eddie, my parents raised two more children. My sister, Helene, was five years younger than I. My brother, Robert, arrived three years after Helene. You would think we would have been close, particularly Helene and I. After all, we were two sisters growing up in a household in which the father yearned for girly girls and the mother left us much to ourselves. But Helene and I never quite connected when we were young. Being five years older, I generally found myself in a different social environment. At times, I wondered if perhaps I should have been paying more attention to Helene. But I had my own friends, and I didn't bother much with her. I can rationalize that I, too, was just trying to find my way through the gauntlet of childhood.

Robert and Helene

I felt some guilt about my relationship with Helene—and regarding my relationship with my father, as compared to hers. We had an intimacy and understanding between us that I don't think ever truly existed between him and Helene. When he killed himself, however, it was Helene who was perhaps most affected. Only eighteen years old, she had been home alone that day, when a couple of uniformed officers arrived to give her the devastating news. She later told me, "The only anchor that I had was gone. I don't think I ever really got over it."

My mother was no anchor for anyone, but even my relationship with her was better than Helene's. My dominant feeling toward her was one of disappointment, but for Helene it was a profound sadness and even some fear. It was clear to my younger sister that our mother didn't care for her. "I expected nothing from her," Helene later said, "and that's what I got." Indeed, I felt very much like the favorite of the family, which is a realization from which nothing good can come for anybody.

As Helene and I matured, I came to realize that life had handed us different and uneven childhood courses. I was very active, very physical, always on the move. She was sickly, suffering from inner ear infections and various minor illnesses, often missing school. It was never anything particularly serious, but she seemed always to be a bit on the margins. Looking back, I often sensed even then that she had made many compromises, and so I often felt a sense of guilt about my accomplishments as compared with my sister's attempts at achievement.

Accomplishments—maybe that's the wrong word. I had advantages over her that I didn't necessarily earn. I recall that summer camp in Maine, for instance. It was a beautiful place. My father visited every summer; I don't recall that my mother ever did. In my early years there, I was treated like the camp mascot. I never forgot what the head counselor, Miss Meyer, said to me one day: "Carolyn, you have the most beautiful lips." There was nothing sinister about the comment. It was just an observation. But I thought, *What does that mean? Beautiful lips? My lips are like anyone else's.* But maybe Helene didn't have the lips, and she didn't have the energy that I enjoyed, and, in fact, she didn't have the camp at Echo Lake. She went to another camp. I remember thinking it was a less impressive one.

I never really understood why Helene seemed to adore me, her less-than-embracing older sister, to the very end. She always called me "Sissy," so much so that her eldest son, whom she named Edward (and to whom I became quite close), called me Aunt Sissy until he began to think better of it by the time he reached law school.

Helene married a physician (they later divorced) and had six children. The third, born with Down's Syndrome, suffered from severe physical and neurological abnormalities and survived only a few years. So Helene and I both survived the loss of a child, albeit under vastly different circumstances. But while I received accolades for my work on behalf of perpetuating Andy's legacy, Helene never quite received the credit she deserved for her efforts. In the wake of her son's death, for instance, she formed a Girl Scout troop for mentally disadvantaged youngsters, and she led it for many years. Years later, her son Ed attended an award ceremony in which a half dozen people were receiving honors for their community service in the White Plains area. He was stunned to discover that his mother had been periodically visiting a prison in Westchester County, where she would read to the prisoners.

Helene wasn't one to tout her accomplishments, and she certainly never grumbled about her setbacks. Indeed, for all the awe she seems to have had for me, her older sister, I am not sure that she realized how much I came to admire *her*. Helene first developed ovarian cancer as early as 1980, when she was only sixty. She was quite ill and quite stoic while suffering through the dreaded surgeries and chemotherapy treatments. The cancer seemed to be in remission, only to return with a vengeance a decade later. Again, more surgery, more chemotherapy. Five years later, it was back once more, but she still endured. Her oncologist was amazed. But when it returned for a fourth time, she was older and frailer, and she finally determined it was time to stop the treatments. It was time to let the disease run its course.

Toward the end, in the autumn of 2001, I visited Helene at her house in White Plains. Ed picked me up at the train station, and we went to see my sister, who was able to sit up in bed and greet people. But she was weak, and it was clear that she wasn't going to recover this time. We spoke for a while and said our goodbyes, that awful moment when you wonder if you'll ever see the person again, yet you want to stave off the thought, leaving your farewells on a note of hope. Still, I was devastated.

After the visit, Ed and I decided to go out for pizza. We didn't talk much during the meal; we were both so sad. It was afterward, during the ten-minute drive back to the train station, that I lost it. I started sobbing. "That should be me," I kept saying. "How come it's not me in that position? Why is it happening to her? I'm older. I've had so much. Your mother's had nothing."

Here I was, always regarded as the stoic one—particularly by Ed, who had always thought of me as confident and controlled (and perhaps a bit controlling). But I just broke down. Ed later admitted he was so shocked by my reaction, a side of me that I didn't share very often, that he almost couldn't drive. But hopefully he gained some insight into my feelings about his mother. Throughout Helene's health struggles, I marveled at her strength and courage and the fact that she never seemed to complain despite having *so much* to complain about. I suppose people said much the same thing about me in the long run, but Helene's battle with cancer, which she finally lost on Christmas Day in 2001, gave me a whole new perspective of my younger sister.

So here was a sort of life lesson that was lifelong in the making. Experience breeds insight. Sometimes you have to develop strength of character to truly recognize the same thing in others. In the end, that little sister whom I so often disregarded in our early years became a sort of heroine to me. I realized it isn't necessarily achievement that inspires, but rather fortitude.

$\mathcal{M}$y younger brother was a different story, actually a sadder tale. Helene and I never had a close relationship with him, and much less so as we grew older. He seemed without an anchor at all, just without any place where he felt like he belonged. Certainly, he didn't feel like a part of the family, and it could have been partially our fault. Maybe we weren't too accepting of him. He was only fifteen when our father died, and shortly thereafter he was gone, too. He just up and left.

Robert never went to college. We didn't know where he was most of the time. He simply traveled the country like a vagabond, wandering here and there. While my memories of my sister revolve around a largely stagnant, indoor childhood, my recollections of my brother are much the opposite. I felt guilty (there's that word again) that I didn't keep in touch with him more after he went away. He wasn't particularly easy to talk to, and he certainly wasn't interested in contacting us. But I felt that I, who was older and more mature in many ways, could have tried harder. His was a very sad and lonely life.

So my lone surviving brother became a vague figure in my world, not unlike my mother in her later years. The last time I saw him was sometime in the 1940s, perhaps a few years after I was married, which is sad to ponder. In the end, of the six people that constituted my family unit as a child, two were lost far too early, and two so distanced themselves from me that the bonds were irrevocably broken. All that remained were Helene and I.

Given my family's dysfunction, it is quite remarkable that my sister and I became as close as we eventually did.

My brother? Well, I heard that at one point he was jailed for bigamy and failure to pay child support. Apparently, he eventually did settle down somewhere in the Midwest, producing a bunch of children with his second wife. One of his daughters actually visited Helene and me in the late 1990s. She was a lovely young woman, and she told me a bit about her father, how he had become very ill and died a few years back, how many siblings and half-siblings she had, what they were all doing. But it was like listening to a story about someone else's family.

I did speak with my brother once after he had clearly removed himself from his familial past. During the conversation, I must have called him Rob, because that's what we called him when I actually knew him. But he quickly said, "Call me Robert." And I think maybe that says it all.

How much of the dysfunction of my first family can be attributed to my parents? Who really knows? Parenting is always trial-and-error. You start out thinking you're very smart. You've talked to people, observed, read books. It is a bit like learning to be a doctor. You can't really be equipped with the proper skills as a physician or a surgeon until you go out into the field and you're confronted with a crisis in need of a quick solution. And it is much the same with parenting. Life is so random, so capricious. You are constantly presented with the unexpected, the unexplored. So as a parent, you constantly improvise. And because circumstances are never quite the same again, what worked once may not work a second time. In that sense, it is a bit like a comedian who offers a punch line. It might have had the audience doubled over in laughter during his first set of the night. But maybe the second time around, his timing is off, or he emphasizes the wrong word, or the crowd is tired late on a Friday night. And nobody laughs. Life, like parenting, is funny that way.

*G*iven the myriad ways in which maturity can transform personality, it was rather amazing years later to consider the evolution of my children and compare it with Bobby's perspective of them as young boys. In a poem he wrote about them when they were ages eight, six, and three, his observations appeared to be right on the mark:

These are my children—these my childlings!
Mine is the zest of their leaping eyes!

Jonny as the thought of a rainbow
Arching the sky in the foam and mist
Piercing the heavens beyond possessing,
Inquiring and prodding and never knowing.
He is Joseph of many colored raiment

He is Quixote of never ending battle
He is Phaeton adrift in his father's chariot
And then a Phoenix emerging from his ashes of longing
Arising from birdling, maturing to eagle
Spreading his wings to fan and rekindle
The sputtered out embers to blistering fire.

And Andy—as the strength of my own excursions
Into the realm of jubilee and laughter
Into the peace of love and beloved
Into the frost of bruise and hurt
Into the fantasy of idols above him
Into the knowledge that good is for him
And from him flows a tide of belonging
That gives to the giver his own desirings.

And David—Here I pause to watch a cataract
Streak like the wild wind across a peopled plain
Scurry in surprise, in adulation, in glory
Tipping the cup of becoming, touching tenderness and pain,
Wandering through valleys that are veins to the mountains
Licking the rocks that are hearts to the brain
Speaking and chortling and frowning and living,
His world as Pandora's wonder—and ours to gain.

Jonathan, the oldest, now is a Hasidic Jew living in Israel, a "Joseph of many colored raiment." A father of seven (and grandfather, too), he so often seems to have his head in the clouds "as the thought of a rainbow," as many talented musicians and artists do. David, the youngest, is a successful businessman in New Jersey who invests in environmental sustainability, power generation, and alternative energy technology—"wandering through valleys that are veins to the mountains." And, of course, Andy, the middle son, became a martyr for the civil rights movement and an icon of a decade's upheaval. He traveled "into the peace of love and beloved, into the frost of bruise and hurt."

David, Andy, and
Jonathan Goodman

But the way each of my children looked or acted or responded or showed certain talents influenced me as a parent, which in turn re-influenced my children. So while we always lived at the apartment on West Eighty-sixth Street, my three sons did not grow up in the same environment at all. The kids were all different, and they came into different homes, led by different parents.

Our prime directives of parenting were to make sure our children knew our feelings, knew our past, and knew their limits. Greatly conscious of what our children gravitated toward and what they excelled at, we would take every opportunity to foster those passions and talents.

We always had a big collection of records in our house, and we had a phonograph placed at a height low enough for a child to use it. When he was quite young, Jonny would take a record and place it on the phonograph. It was, in fact, just about the only thing that kept him quiet. He was two or three years old at the time, and he didn't necessarily know what he was listening to, but he loved the act of listening. He would also fiddle around on the piano, his little fingers roaming the black and white keys. Something was obviously drawing Jonny to music.

When he grew a bit older, we set him up with piano lessons. Of course, like most children, Jonny never liked to practice; he just wanted to play. But he developed such an ear for music, such an appreciation of the art form as informed by his passions. Later, one of my own great passions became attending concerts with him because he heard things that most people wouldn't have heard. Much like how Bobby used to make a poem come alive or, much later, how at an art museum my second husband, Joe, would approach a painting I had seen dozens of times and point out qualities in it that made me wonder if I'd ever seen it before. Such a thing was always magical to me—artistic insight.

When your first child is born—hopefully one you wanted to have very much—that child is the center of your world, the center of your attentions. So it was with us. But Andy, the second-born, didn't get the same kind of time from his parents, simply as a result of the altered family dynamic. In contrast with Jonny, a gorgeous child with blond hair and beautiful features, Andy was not a particularly attractive baby. He had little wisps of dark hair. People who visited would sort of look at Andy for a few moments, then they would rush over to Jonny. I think that influences a parent's attitudes, to some extent. Indeed, all parents sense but few are willing to admit such differences of feeling regarding their children. I know that I was partial to Jonny in the beginning, in part because he showed so much musical talent.

To Jonny, music is a connection to God. He tells of how Brahms and Beethoven would explain that their finest compositions didn't come *from* them, but rather *through* them. Jonny seeks the purity in music, so perhaps it should come as no surprise that he embarked on a search for true religion in his life—as opposed to what he considered his artificial upbringing as a reform Jew whose bar mitzvah was a "lip service joke."

When Andy was killed, Jonny was enrolled in the Juilliard Graduate School as a conductor, a tremendous accomplishment. The practical aspects of music always interested him, but he soon began to chafe at the notion of having to go through an academic gauntlet just to prove himself as an artist. After nearly four years there, he decided he wasn't interested in getting a degree after all. So he left. And he opted for religion instead.

"Mom," he said to me one day, "I've decided I better find out what it means to be a Jew." He had heard a calling, a need to embark on a search for spiritual discovery: "Piercing the heavens beyond possessing . . . Inquiring and prodding and never knowing," as his father had written so many years before.

So in the mid-1960s, Jonny began visiting a local yeshiva and wearing a Star of David. He started spending a great deal of time at a kosher restaurant on the Lower East Side and eventually joined the Chabad-Lubavitch movement, a branch of Hasidism. Finally, he told me, "I think I have to go to Israel." That was where his search took him, and when he was nearly forty years old that's where he decided he needed to live his life. Jonny remains there—in K'far Chabad, a Lubavitch village about a half hour by bus from Tel Aviv—and he speaks Hebrew most of the time, such that he occasionally stumbles over word selection when forced to speak English. He has worked as an arranger and composer of religious music, even putting out a handful of CDs, and as a recording technician, still interested in the practical aspects of music. But mostly he has devoted himself to being a Jew.

Some, myself included, were certain that Jonny's conversion was a reaction to Andy's death, a tragedy that he found particularly meaningless. After all, the word "Lubavitch" in Russian means "city of brotherly love." Still, Jonny insists it isn't true, that my interpretation was an attempt to find some sort of reason for his decision, a choice I never quite understood. But I did come to accept it.

Indeed, even though I was at odds with his whole outlook on things when he became profoundly religious, Jonny claims that his change actually improved our relationship. We didn't always see eye to eye about many things as he entered adulthood, but after his conversion (or perhaps it was an evolution) I think we each came to an epiphany. For my part, I realized that his beliefs, however different from mine, didn't change the fact that I loved him, that he was my son. If tolerance, after all, was my calling, then I had to admit that he had the right to decide what was best for him and who he was, and I had to respect that choice. And Jonny came to realize that the Torah calls on us to honor our father and mother. "I discovered," he later explained, "that this was a person with whom I wanted to have a relationship, probably more than anybody else in the world."

Our mother–son bond became almost a do-over, a remake. I visited him and his seven children and grandchildren often in Israel. Occasionally, he would find his way to New York to see me. And perhaps, in that geography, there lies a metaphor about our relationship. We didn't meet halfway. We remained as stubborn as ever in our disparate beliefs. But we came to understand that love can bridge any divide.

Surely, my interpretation of Jonny's transformation—that it was a reaction to devastation about Andy—was rooted in the fact that his younger brother had developed such a winning personality. Andy was always so tuned in to what was happening in the world, which is why he related so well to so many things and so many people. And, of course, he grew into a handsome young man. He began to look so much like my husband, which was endlessly enchanting to me. I would watch him walk down the street and think to myself, *There goes a miniature Bobby*. Ask anyone who is happily married, and I would guess that most would admit to being particularly captivated by the child who looks most like their spouse. But then Andy was captivating to just about everybody.

*A*fter two boys, I wanted a daughter. In fact, I had a name picked out for my little girl—my middle name, Elizabeth. I had always believed girls were supposed to be especially close to their mothers (my own history notwithstanding). That's how it was in books and movies and in the general experience of many people I knew. I remember when Andy was born, and the nurse told me I had another son; I replied, "Another boy?" Then when my third son, David, was born, I gave up on that particular dream. I figured if I had five or six children, they would all be boys. So I desperately yearned for the kind of relationship I had never known. I thought I needed a girl for that. But it turns out I didn't. David became that person.

Ironically so, in a sense, because as the third child he probably got less attention than the other two. Perhaps that's partly why David learned independence very early in life. Bobby and I always felt that parenting was more about quality than quantity. Bobby's work took him away quite a bit early on, especially when Jonny was young. And I, too, was pulled in various directions. I was never really a full-time mother in the traditional sense. We had help around the house, and if I happened to be busy with something, somebody else would pick the children up at school.

One day, however, when I did pick up David at school his teacher said, "You know, I haven't seen you much lately." I told him that, yes, I was busy. I was going to school myself at the time, earning a master's degree in clinical psychology from the City University of New York.

"Yeah," said a six-year-old David, who has always been one to speak his mind. "It keeps her out of trouble."

I don't know why people are who they are, but David always had an awareness of the monetary value of things. He was a businessman from Day One, unlike his father and his brothers. Bobby was a wonderful engineer, but I can't say he was a great businessman. Neither is Jonny, the musician who struggles to make ends meet. Nor was Andy. That difference between Andy and David is evident in their approach to baseball cards. Andy would spend his ten cents on chewing gum— not for the gum but for the three baseball cards that came with it. He was trying to collect the whole card series and, frankly, not doing too well at it.

Then one day, the doorbell rang. David stood there holding a box so big he'd been unable to open the door. The box was filled with baseball cards. He had negotiated them off of a wealthy friend of his who apparently had no use for them. David had no use for them, either, but that didn't matter.

"Mom," he said, his arms full, "these are for Andy."

His older brother was delighted, obviously, at such a windfall—thrilled to now own a box full of Stan Musials and Warren Spahns and Roy Campanellas. And David was delighted, too, because he had made the deal. He was the big shot little brother.

For years after Andy was gone, I kept those baseball cards in my bedroom closet. But at a certain point, I thought, *My gosh, what do I need these for?* So I threw them out, just impulsively dumped them in the garbage. Subsequently, I learned how much they would be worth these days. Apparently, David could have taught his mother a thing or two.

Actually, David did. He taught me, somewhat paradoxically, that independence can coexist with intimacy.

One lesson was learned in Paris. Both of my older boys traveled to Europe, but not with me. However, David and I traveled to the continent together when he was twelve. Just the two of us. How many other preteen boys would do that? I remember we had packed two large bags, but David seemed to be wearing the same clothes every day.

"Why don't you change your clothes?" I asked. He told me he didn't have much to change into.

"Then what's in your bag?"

He showed me. It was his stamp collection. He told me he wanted to bring his albums to the stamp market in Paris. Again, there was that business acumen. He knew the value of things. And I knew, because he had learned independence early on, that I could leave him. I told him I wanted to visit the Louvre. I pointed to a nearby bench and told him to meet me at that exact spot precisely at noon.

So I visited the Louvre, where I unexpectedly ran into some cousins of mine. How often does that happen four thousand miles from home? We went to a café, got to talking . . . and suddenly I realized I was late to meet my son. I was panicked. *My little boy doesn't know where his mother is. He doesn't speak French. He's lost in Paris.* I grabbed a cab and dashed to our meeting spot, only to find David seated on the bench with his arm resting comfortably behind the back of an elderly, white-haired lady. I ran to him and began to apologize profusely.

"That's all right," he said. "Meet Mrs. Rubenstein."

David had heard her speaking English and French and had asked her to translate while he traded stamps. After finishing, they had discovered a series of mutual acquaintances while sitting without a care in the world on that bench. So there was David, not at all concerned that his mother was a half hour late.

Despite being so comfortable out on his own, David had a knack for profoundly personal and thoughtful gestures. I used to wear these marvelous hats. I suppose I was sort of known for that. One had a stiff lace brim, its crown adorned in colorful wild flowers. David told me, "Mom, when we're traveling— whether we're in an airport or a bus station or some strange place—always wear that hat, and I'll find you wherever you are." Earlier, on one lovely spring afternoon, David and I had been walking along Madison Avenue when I stopped to look in the window of a hat shop. And I just stared at that hat. Frankly, if I were with my other two boys, they would have said, "C'mon, Mom. Let's go!" Which is what most boys would do. But David, who was probably about nine years old, peered into the window and then turned his face up to me. "Mom," he said, "why don't we go inside so you can try it on?"

Such depths of emotion can attach to a hat or a phonograph or a clarinet, tales behind the tools and trinkets that stayed vivid in my memory for decades. A favorite example of David's caring concerns a doll, though it happened when David was all grown up.

One late spring in the early 1950s, Bobby had gone ahead to Tupper Lake with the boys. He had just finished constructing part of the thruway, and he wanted to show them the road. I left the following day, along with a lovely woman named Emma whom we had hired as a housekeeper. The car was filled to the brim with trunks, duffel bags, all sorts of things. We made it all the way to North Creek, a small town in the Adirondacks still some sixty miles from Tupper Lake. All of a sudden, I caught the scent of something. It was pungent but pleasant, or at least I thought so at first. "Oh, what a wonderful smell!" I said to Emma. "There must be bread baking somewhere around here." Well, it wasn't bread. We went another few miles, and the smell came along, too. Then the car started wobbling, and I pulled to the side of the road. We had a flat tire.

Here we were on the outskirts of a blink-and-you-miss-it town along a sparsely traveled stretch of road in the middle of the infrequently visited Adirondacks. Most of the area resorts weren't even open for the season yet. It wasn't yet dark, but it was growing late, and squadrons of tiny midges were beginning to come out in force. I managed to locate a wrench after unloading the duffels and trunks packed atop the toolbox. And I just stood there, trying to figure out what to do.

It's funny, really. You can live a life of achievement—huddle with icons, hobnob with the rich and famous and truly inspirational, speak to myriad young people with the authority of someone who has been on intimate terms with the best and worst of humanity's potential. But that doesn't mean you can change a tire. Life is humbling that way.

In my experience, however, humbling moments seem to be the times when fate points you in a certain direction. When you're a bit lost, unsure of the next move, wondering if perhaps you took a wrong turn somewhere along the way, something unexpected tends to come along. In this case, it was a fellow in a pickup truck.

"Lady, you look like you're in trouble. Can I help you?"

"You sure can," I replied. Surely my voice trembled with excitement at having been saved from what was starting to look like the beginning of a low-budget horror movie: *Attack of the Midges*!

As he started to change the tire, I thought to myself, *I'll give him a few dollars.*

"What are you doing around here?" I wondered.

"Well," he said, continuing to work on the tire, "my wife and daughter and I make these little birch bark canoes and Indian dolls out of deerskin. And we sew beads on them. And we make baskets. I sell them to the resorts." Then he turned to me, "I want you to know that a one hundred percent American is changing your tire."

I thought, *Oh, God! Of all the people to stop, I have to get a McCarthyite.* But he didn't look the type.

"What exactly do you mean?"

"I'm an American Indian," he said. "Mohawk tribe."

I figured this man might be too proud to accept a couple of bucks from me. So instead I said, "Can I buy some of those?"

Paying him for a bunch of baskets and dolls and little birch bark canoes, I placed them in the back of the station wagon. Then he and I merrily parted ways. When I finally arrived at

Tupper Lake and made my way down to the boathouse, where Bobby and the kids were staying, everybody looked anxious and worried. Bobby was beside himself, knowing that his usually prompt wife was an hour and a half late. Then he looked in the back of the car, and he was furious.

"I'm here worrying myself to death," he said, "and you're out shopping?"

But that isn't the end of the tale. This story is about David. I gave away most of those Native American artifacts, but it turned out that I kept one of the dolls for years. Some four decades later, when the house at Tupper Lake was being sold, David went up there to look around, to see if there was anything he thought I might like to have. About six months later, I came home one night after celebrating my birthday, and I could barely squeeze through my door. The whole foyer and front hall of the apartment were filled with vases and pots of blooming chrysanthemums. *Who brought these?* I wondered. That's when I noticed the little Native American doll right in front of this gorgeous array of flowers. For me, it represented not only my memories of Tupper Lake, but my son's thoughtfulness and his understanding of what really mattered to me.

It always served as a source of pride for me that my sons emulated different characteristics of their parents and chose their own widely diverging paths accordingly. But as different as they are and always will be—and Jonny and David could not be much more distinct in their chosen ways of life—they care greatly about both distant injustices and the people to whom they are the closest. Andy was like that, too.

LETTER FROM PHILADELPHIA

June 24, 1942

Dear Jonathan,

Now that your vocabulary has reached the extensive proportions of many words and varied intonations, and the expression in your wonderful eyes so filled with your own particular meanings, I think it time we started to correspond with one another. I'll write the first letter and you don't, unless you wish to, have to answer until you're off and away to college. And even then, should the press of higher learning consume too much of your time, I won't mind if you don't write me as much as I might wish, just so long as you still smile as you do now, and so long as you leap about the world with the joy of living, of discovering new things, of experimenting with your mind through the exciting maze of the world's way. The important thing for both of us, Jonny, is to keep the spirit you now possess turned toward making the best of what we find around us, not by acquiescing to all things as they are because it is too difficult to mold them closer to our own desire, but by seeing our life as a constant struggle with complacency everywhere.

Look how I drift off with speculations and fatherly advice the first time I try to speak to you in your newly acquired tongue. I'll try to stay away from too much serious finger lifting with the long classic expression that has come down to us from Victorian days of parent lecturing son when he was about to set off to the big city to "earn his fortune." But sometimes your own love drives in a surge of wonder, and you just can't help talking about life and its meaning.

It all came about tonight while I was walking about the streets of the town Ben Franklin made, narrow old world streets with hitching posts every ten feet in some places, red brick walks with a lively green grass coming up between the spaces that have accumulated dust since our first revolution. I felt quite alone here away from your mother and you, pacing the streets with dreams of our world, the three of us, glad when this war is over, and full of schemes to make our land better than it ever has been before. There shadows sloping down from the windows, streaks of light disturbing the darkness. Here and there, someone would raise a blind and look down at me and wonder who the stranger below was and what thoughts were drifting through his head. Some homes had doors that would creak on aged hinges, complaining of centuries of mis-use and certainly no care. And then there were all kinds of stores with windows darkened for the night, antique shops, metal ware shops with cozy corners and odd shapes and goblin fancies in the room beyond I couldn't see.

There were many things to buy, Jonny boy, things to fix when they fell apart, toys belonging to other boys now as old as your father sitting here in his room in Philadelphia thinking of the time he would play with games even as you will do, and thinking perhaps that some of the old balls and blocks and bats had found their joyous way through the hands of other boys into the little shop that poor Richard might have founded. Everything inside belonged to you because every boy that ever played with the sundry things inside found happiness in pursuits within his own understanding, even as you do now with your hauntingly beautiful little soul.

Your dad.

FOOTSTEPS

$\mathcal{A}$ndy was at Queens College in the spring of 1964 when Fanny Lou Hamer and Aaron Henry of the Mississippi Freedom Democratic Party were recruiting northern students for the Mississippi Summer Project, which became widely known as Freedom Summer. After graduating from high school, Andy actually had enrolled at the University of Wisconsin. But he wound up contracting pneumonia during his first semester and left school, returning to New York and assisting his father in construction of the Alexander Hamilton Bridge. He then transferred to Queens, in part because he was drawn to the drama department. Theater arts were his first love, and he acted in off Broadway productions. He also studied anthropology and political science. Those were his interests—history, histrionics, and humanity.

Andy had been moved to action by the black-and-white images bursting from the television in the previous year—the tanks and dogs and fire hoses in Birmingham, the church bombing and four young bodies buried. Summer volunteers were required to have at least $500, just in case they had to bail themselves out of jail in Mississippi. So Andy began rising early every morning to work loading trucks for United Parcel Service. He wanted to pay his own way if he was accepted into the program.

Upon his acceptance, Andy went to train in Oxford, Ohio. Soon, he was scheduled to make use of that training in Canton, Mississippi, which amounted to a somewhat safe assignment, at least relative to other scenarios. But his older brother, Jonathan, knew that if Andy was going south and there was a dangerous mission, he would volunteer. "You're going to pick the riskiest place to go," Jonny predicted. "That's your nature." Andy didn't think about what might happen to him; he thought about what needed to be done. I was always the same way, I suppose. Do I wish my son had been different from me? I doubt it.

What Bobby and I tried to do, basically, was act as role models for our children. Lead by example. For instance, during the years of widespread unionization, we were very sympathetic to the unions, and we stood on the picket lines with them. So we were involved in what we believed in. We would tell our children, essentially, that if you believe in something in the interest of social or economic justice, it is one thing to support it and talk about it. But if you really care about a situation, you get out there and do what you can. In the words of Martin Luther King, Jr., "An individual has not started living until he can rise above the narrow confines of his individualistic concerns to the broader concerns of all humanity."

Perhaps my activist tendencies could be traced back to 1923 in Queens. I was seven years old, and, curious child that I was, I had become well-acquainted with my family's gardener. He was a good man, a family man, but somewhere along the line he must have hinted that his job forced him to be away from his children too often. So I convinced him to ask his customers (my father included) for a raise so that he could spend more time with his family. Fortunately, my father wasn't too upset. He wouldn't have been. After all, he had hired one of the first black attorneys to work at a white New York law firm. That sort of thing inspires a little girl to a life of trying to do the right thing.

Many newspaper and magazine articles about me over the years described me as having leftist political inclinations. One reporter even asked if I had once been a "card-carrying" member of the Communist Party. I found all of this categorization rather silly. Although I became strongly supportive of members of the Upper West Side Democratic Party, at various times I voted for Republicans and Independents as well. Party affiliation didn't interest me; I worried most about a candidate's views and qualifications. Of course, if believing in our constitutional constructs is considered left wing, then I was proudly that for all of my adult life.

At Cornell in the 1930s, Bobby and I helped organize local farmers' cooperatives. These dairy farmers were taking beatings—financially and, sometimes, physically. They were practically giving their products away to big businesses, despite having to labor from dawn to dusk and having to spend money on feed and care of their cattle. We went out there and asked them, "How much are you selling your milk for? What is it costing you? What do you think they're selling the milk for?" They had no idea. They were innocents back then, and it seemed that our primary responsibility toward them was one of education. Critics, who always abound, wondered why we city slickers were involved. But we just wanted to inform them of their rights.

During that time, we also were involved in aiding Spanish Republicans who fled or were exiled by Francisco Franco during the Spanish Civil War. I "adopted" a Spanish child, raising money to provide for her and her family. I don't recall her name, but I remember her face, especially her big and beautiful eyes. I kept her photograph for years.

Bobby and I were strong supporters of the people who had the courage to battle the Spanish Nationalists. International brigades from all over Europe had formed to fight Franco and the Nationalists, who were supported by Nazi Germany and fascist Italy. Several units had American components, which came to be loosely referred to as the Abraham Lincoln Brigade. Although the cause was eventually lost, the courageous participants were still forced to fight for many years after—for their own freedom on American soil. The House Un-American Activities Committee (HUAC) became a backyard fascist organization.

One of the victims of the witch hunt was Dr. Edward Barsky. A remarkable man, Barsky went to Spain in the 1930s and took charge of the medical services of the International Brigade, organizing seven hospitals and performing daring frontline surgery while under fire from Hitler-supplied artillery. By all rights, he should have been welcomed home as a hero, someone who fought for the very freedoms trumpeted by so-called American patriots.

Following the Spanish Civil War, Barsky led the work of organizing the Joint Anti-Fascist Refugee Committee (JAFRC), which lobbied U.S. leadership on behalf of the deposed Republican government and cared for some 150,000 Spanish Republican refugees. (I eventually became Women's Division Chair of the JAFRC.) When McCarthyism reared its ugly head, Barsky refused to give the committee's records to HUAC because he knew that their publication would place in jeopardy all persons in Franco's Spain who were related to those being aided. As a result, he and ten colleagues were charged with contempt of Congress and sent to prison. Barsky's six-month sentence being the longest. Even worse, his medical license was later suspended, and the constitutionality of that course of action was later upheld by the Supreme Court. But I agreed with Justice William O. Douglas's dissenting opinion: "When a doctor cannot save lives in America because he is opposed to Franco in Spain, it is time to call a halt and look critically at the neurosis that has possessed us."

At the height of anti-Communist fervor in 1951, we thumbed our noses at HUAC and raised bail money by throwing a farewell party for Barsky and his colleagues. It wasn't a particularly unusual sort of gathering for us. Our home on Eighty-sixth Street became a haven for the progressive actors, writers, musicians, and intellectuals who populated Manhattan's Upper West Side, especially McCarthy targets like Alger Hiss, actor Zero Mostel, novelist Howard Fast, and my good friend Martin Popper, an attorney who defended the blacklisted Hollywood Ten and became our family's spokesperson after Andy's disappearance. Many of the people whom we hosted lost jobs and had to flee prosecution; some were even harassed to the point of committing suicide.

People often wondered why so many books lined the walls of our apartment, many of them duplicate copies. Well, a good number of them were cookbooks. I had scores of them on the bookshelves in my kitchen, some written by my friends like Carolyn Dearman (wife of former *Neshoba Democrat* editor and

Mississippi hero Stanley Dearman) and Katy Popper (wife of Martin Popper). I needed them if I was going to host these huge gatherings. But many of the books in the apartment weren't ours. They were left-leaning reading material of friends who were frightened, figuring it was better not to have socialist "evidence" lying around their houses. So they gave the books to us. It became a library representing fear and disillusionment.

But on this day, in 1951, we attempted to put a whimsical spin on a tragic situation by throwing what we called a "birthday party" for Dr. Barsky. The local baker's union made a big cake, which we placed in the dining room. The most lasting image that night came when the guest of honor prepared to leave, his destination being prison. There in the doorway stood seven-year-old Andy, whom we had sent to the progressive Walden School in Manhattan because a public education would not allow the freedom to discuss the current oppressive state of the union. Andy was learning tolerance and compassion, but it seemed to be innate with him anyway. He stood there in the doorway his head bowed, tears rolling down his face.

"What's wrong?" somebody asked.

"It just seems so mean," he sobbed, "to make people go to jail on their birthday."

So should I have been surprised that Andy went to Mississippi? He was merely following in our footsteps with courage and without hesitation.

Bobby and Carolyn at the
Women's Strike for Peace, 1967

When the Mount Zion Methodist Church in rural Neshoba County's all-black community of Longdale was firebombed by a gang of armed and hooded men in mid-June 1964, the arsonists came looking for one man in particular: twenty-four-year-old Congress of Racial Equality field staff worker Mickey Schwerner. Mickey had spoken at Mount Zion only three days earlier, urging the congregation to register to vote. "You have been slaves too long," he had said. "We can help you help yourselves." To the members of the Mississippi White Knights of the Ku Klux Klan, he was public enemy number one. The Klan called him "Goatee" for the beard he grew to make himself look older. He was the outside agitator, the New York Jew, who represented everything the entrenched South despised about the civil rights movement.

In January of that year, Mickey and his wife, Rita, had driven from Manhattan to the city of Meridian in Lauderdale

County, on the southern border of Neshoba County. They ran a local community center for the area's black residents, the first of its kind in Meridian, and within six months it made a significant impact on the community. They quickly befriended a twenty-one-year-old black man named James Chaney, who had spent his life in Mississippi gritting his teeth against his second-class status. He would become Mickey's closest colleague. Their combined success earned them the enmity of the area Klansmen, whose numbers had skyrocketed as the civil rights struggle intensified. The Schwerners, in particular, received dozens of menacing phone calls and religious and racial slurs. They were tailed by cars, repeatedly picked up for questioning by police, eventually even evicted from their home. I always marveled at their courage, their dedication to values so enduring that they would risk their lives daily in what amounted to a foreign land.

Then the church burned. Mickey and James were in Ohio at the Freedom Summer training grounds when they heard the news. They asked for volunteers, outlining the inherent dangers in the area but emphasizing the overwhelming need. Andy offered to go with them. When he phoned me to explain why he was going to east-central Mississippi, a particularly entrenched area of the state where southern values were defended by any means necessary, my heart sank. I remembered Jonny's words. But I concealed my fears, afraid I would dissolve in tears.

That was the last conversation I ever had with Andy, the last real conversation, though ever after I spoke to him and of him often.

Later, I came across a poem Andy had written some weeks earlier for a poetry course at Queens College. The professor subsequently told me how much Andy meant to her in that class, which consisted almost entirely of young men, most of them too macho to open up and reveal their innermost thoughts. But there was Andy, handsome and strong, and he would boldly stand and recite a poem with such conviction and such emotion that the other men were inspired to follow suit. At one point, the class discussed A.E. Housman's "An Athlete Dying Young," and Andy submitted his own version, which he called "Corollary to a Poem by A.E. Housman":

How dismally the day
Screams out and blasts the night.
What disaster you will say,
To start another fight.

See how heaven shows dismay
As her stars are scared away;
As the sun ascends with might
With his hot and awful light.

He shows us babies crying
We see the black boy dying
We close our eyes and choke our sighs
And look into the dreadful skies.

Then peacefully the night
Puts out the reddened day
And the jaws that used to bite
Are sterile where we lay.

Andrew Goodman, May 1964

A SHORT WHILE
TOWARDS THE SUN

$\mathcal{S}$ince childhood, I had always been in love with the stage, and I spent a few years acting in a community theater near Woodmere. One play in particular remained vivid in my memory. It was an antiwar drama called "Bury the Dead" in which, as a teenager, I played the mother of a dead soldier. At one point, in a surreal setting, I stood on stage in a state of denial that my son had been injured while a group of soldiers crouched below me in a trench. One of them was the actor playing my son.

"Let me see your face, son," was my line. And I repeated it over and over. "Let me see your face, son."

Finally, he turned to me, showing me the little that was left of his face. He was dead. All the men in the trench were dead. My response was to scream. I did, and a primordial sound came out, remarkably heartfelt and drenched in emotion. I screamed that scream over and over every weekend.

Some three decades later, on Sunday, June 21, 1964, my son disappeared. It was Father's Day and only Andy's second day in Mississippi. The longest day of the year became the longest day of my life.

Having driven all night from Ohio before going to examine what was left of the Mount Zion Methodist Church, Andy, Mickey, and James had not returned. We received a phone call that night from members of the Student Nonviolent Coordinating Committee, who explained their hard and fast rule that everyone was supposed to be back before dark. Here it was, late at night, and nobody had heard from them. Nobody knew where they were.

The very first day of Freedom Summer, and three volunteers were already missing in Mississippi. The fact that my son was one of them shook me to my soul. But I didn't allow the dark possibilities in the back of my mind to creep into my thinking. Not yet, at least. As Bobby once wrote to me, "It's still as Freud put it—to know a thing and to accept firmly in your own mind the truth of what you know are such opposite poles of realization that this simple process has become one of the most difficult elements in human endeavor and the root of all personal failure."

The following day, a phone call to the Neshoba County jail revealed that Andy, Mickey, and James had been arrested the previous afternoon for speeding in their blue Ford station wagon. They hadn't been seen since. The FBI, having already begun a church arson investigation, became intensely involved, eventually devoting 153 men to the case. When officials began searching in the swamps and forests of Mississippi, they didn't find the bodies of my son and his colleagues. But they did find a number of other bodies—local African-Americans who had gone missing over the years. It was that kind of place and that kind of time, suffering from that kind of inequality between the resources and attention given blacks and whites.

Within two days, the case had begun to galvanize the country, so much so that Bobby and I, along with Mickey's father Nathan Schwerner, flew to Washington, D.C., where President Lyndon Johnson personally greeted us and told us he would do everything in his power to find our sons. When we returned home, not long after we walked into the house, President Johnson called to tell us that an abandoned, badly burned, blue Ford station wagon had been found in a swamp thirteen miles northeast of Philadelphia, Mississippi.

I screamed in agony. This time it was real.

That same day, we received a postcard Andy had mailed upon arriving in Mississippi. He had been told to write us a positive message. That way, no matter who read it, they would get no revealing information. For decades, the card remained on my mantelpiece:

Dear mom and Dad

    I have arrived safely in Meridian Mississippi. This is a wonderful town and the weather is fine. I wish you were here. The people in this city are wonderful and our reception was very good.

        All my love
           Andy

For the next six weeks, dozens of reporters would crowd into our living room or gather in front of the building on Eighty-sixth Street, day after day, as I gave interview after interview, pleading to the people of Philadelphia, of Mississippi, of anywhere really, for help in tracking down my son. As the days passed, I still managed to generate a flicker of hope that perhaps Andy and Mickey and James were simply being kept somewhere, held out of sight. Most of the young people with whom we were in contact knew they were dead, but I didn't allow myself to think that way. I couldn't.

Bobby and I managed to endure somehow, in part because we rarely had time to ourselves—time when we could truly reflect on the horror of the situation. Our house was full of people—not only the media, but also friends and family providing constant support. And FBI agents, who were providing constant surveillance. They would sit in a back room, tapping our phones with primitive recording equipment. And, in fact, we received a number of detestable phone calls from people demanding ransom in return for my son. No lead led anywhere.

Forty-four days after they went missing, Bobby and I tried to ease our pain with music in the form of a concert at Lincoln Center. There, in the middle of a performance, a friend came rushing down the aisle and pulled us from the auditorium. They had found the bodies. On August 4, the FBI, acting on an informant's tip, bulldozed an earthen dam on the outskirts of Philadelphia and uncovered the very scene I had been dreading most.

The following day was Bobby's fiftieth birthday. Somehow he managed to get through a public statement that encapsulated our grief, our expectations, and our continued values:

The passage of many weeks of uncertainty has ended in the knowledge of the murder of our son Andrew Goodman and his companions, James Chaney and Michael Schwerner. Hope, slim though it was, has passed away and a painful certainty has come. Our grief, though personal, belongs to our nation. This tragedy is not private. It is part of the public conscience of our country.

It is necessary, especially in such a time of agony, to confront ourselves with our own history and the social sickness that still remains long after 'the binding together of our nation's wounds' that was our Civil War. The values our son expressed in his simple action of going to Mississippi are still the bonds that bind this nation together—its Constitution, its law, its Bill of Rights. Whenever and wherever part of a people mock our heritage, as has now and again been done, we must respond with the full power and strength of our heritage. The solution of this crime and punishment of those who have committed it is necessary as part of the process that will enable this nation to endure.

Throughout our history, countless Americans have died in the continuing struggle for equality. We shall continue to work for this goal, and we fervently hope that Americans so engaged will be aided and protected in this noble mission. For ourselves, we wish to express our pride in our son's commitment and that of his companions now dead; and that of his companions now alive, now in Mississippi, acting each hour to express those truths that are self-evident.

In Washington four weeks ago, my wife and I in a sense made a pilgrimage to the Lincoln Memorial in the evening, and stood in that great shrine looking down past the Washington Monument toward the soft glow of the light around the White House. Full of the awe of a great nation that surrounded us, we turned to read, emblazoned in black letters on the white marble, "It is for us the living to dedicate ourselves that these dead shall not have died in vain."

The story that emerged of how they died—painstakingly pieced together by Seth Cagin and Philip Dray in their book

We Are Not Afraid—was awful, not only in its violence and the devastation of so many lives, but also in the series of what-ifs. After the trio had driven away from the church that day, they had a choice when they reached Highway 16: a twenty-five-mile route straight to Meridian, or a longer one through Philadelphia. They chose the latter, perhaps believing it to be safer. If they had chosen otherwise, they might all still be alive today.

As they drove toward Philadelphia, Neshoba County deputy sheriff Cecil Ray Price passed them going the other way. He made a U-turn, having recognized the station wagon, and caught up with them just inside the city limits. Price was a Klansman, not a rarity in Mississippi law enforcement in those days, and he was eager to impress his friends by stopping Mickey Schwerner and his colleagues. He arrested James for speeding, and he apparently told Andy and Mickey that they would be held as suspects in the church arson.

It was more than six hours later that the three were finally released from their jail cells. They hadn't been allowed to make phone calls, but Mickey had previously instructed a colleague to call every jail and sheriff's office along their planned route if they hadn't arrived by 4:00 that afternoon. The Neshoba County Jail received a call at 5:30. No, came the lie, the men hadn't been seen all day.

Caution had been a significant part of the training for the Mississippi volunteers. They were given tips: Don't give a sniper a target by standing in an open window. Know the roads in and out of town. Beware of cars without license plates and policemen without badges. And don't go anywhere at night. But when Andy, Mickey, and James were released (James having paid a $20 fine), they left anyway without making a phone call, a sure signal that something was wrong. James drove south on Highway 19 toward Meridian. Unbeknownst to my son and his friends, Price and Sheriff Lawrence Rainey were involved in a plan to ambush them.

Two carloads of Ku Klux Klan members took off after them. One car broke down; the other kept going, joined by Price in his police cruiser. Eventually, not far from the Lauderdale County line, Price caught up and turned on his lights. James made the fateful decision to pull over. Andy, Mickey, and James—to me, they weren't the "three civil rights workers," as they became forever known; they were Andy and Mickey and James—were placed in the backseat of Price's cruiser. He and the other Klansmen, one of them driving the station wagon, turned around and headed back toward Philadelphia. But before reaching the city, they turned left at an unlit, unmarked dirt road and stopped. "So you wanted to come to Mississippi," one of the Klansmen reportedly said. "Well, now we're gonna let you stay here."

Mickey was killed first, shot in the heart. Andy was second. James was last, and he may have been severely beaten, too. They were buried under ten tons of dirt in a dam being constructed to create a cattle pond. Forty-four days later—after the FBI became involved while suspecting law enforcement officials, after the story had made front-page headlines throughout the country, after Sheriff Rainey had continued his sickening swagger and his contention that it was all a hoax, and after an unidentified citizen was paid $30,000 in reward money to reveal where the bodies were buried—the bodies were finally unearthed. Andy's left hand was clutching soil that could have come only from the dam site, meaning he may still have been alive when buried.

That is how my son died.

Fannie Lee Chaney, Carolyn Goodman,
Anne Schwerner, August 9, 1964

$\mathcal{I}$ gave one last press conference in the apartment, rather numbly thanking the people from all over the nation for the many supportive letters we had received. Then the lights turned off, and one by one, the reporters and cameramen and technicians shuffled up to me at the front of the living room and offered their condolences. Many years later, longtime WNBC correspondent Gabe Pressman remarked that in his more than sixty-year career he had never seen that before or after.

The Schwerners wanted to bury their son next to his friend, James, in Meridian. But the state would not permit it. Even death, it seems, was segregated in Mississippi. We wanted Andy to be buried in New York, next to his grandfather, Charles, who had died only the previous year. When the body was shipped north, we had a simple funeral. The mourners filled the funeral parlor, but it wasn't like the memorial service we had later, where the crowds spilled out into the streets of Manhattan.

I walked in, and there was the casket. And something happened.

When the boys were young, we used to take them on long car trips, often up to Tupper Lake. Andy had loved play-acting from the time he was a little boy, long before he became involved with the theater. We would be in the car, and Andy would reach back, grab whatever clothes were strewn about the car, and try them on. I recall one time in particular when he dressed up in an oversized sweater, a colorful scarf, and the funniest little hat. He was probably four or five years old, and he looked so darling, so funny, so alive.

I had never had a hallucination before and haven't since, but when I walked into the funeral parlor that day I swear I saw Andy sitting on top of that coffin, cross-legged, dressed up as I had remembered him so many years earlier. I don't know why, at that moment in my grieving, I remembered Andy as a five-year-old. I know I wanted him to be alive, to be a young, carefree innocent again. I wanted to remember the loveliness of Andy Goodman. I wanted him to be with me, not in that . . . box.

Whatever the mind does in such situations, when I saw the coffin of my son, my dead twenty-year-old son, I suddenly saw the loving smile of a little boy.

We later held Andy's memorial service at the New York Society for Ethical Culture on West Central Park Avenue, and the eulogizers, though each was devastated by the loss of Andy, were remarkably eloquent. They managed to allow a glimpse of hope and inspiration into a very dark moment.

Andy's best friend, Ralph Engelman: "In going to Mississippi, Andy risked not only death but dying in vain. Whether the most important and publicized domestic crisis since President Kennedy's assassination will quickly disappear from the public consciousness or whether it will become a small watershed in American history remains to be seen. But the significance Andy's sacrifice will assume in the years to come will be a sure barometer of the fate of the cause for which he gave his life. . . . Andy has retaught us an old truth: that although we live and die alone, our personal happiness and destinies are inextricably linked; that none of us is free unless all are free; that we must demand not only comfort but also justice; and that there will always exist those superior souls such as Andy to remind us of these truths."

Rabbi Arthur Lelyveld: "There are those, the rabbis assure us, who earn the kingdom in an hour, for a life is not judged by its length. Andy, who will be part of all that is swift and loving and brave and beautiful forever, won his kingdom in an hour. To die in a cause so pure is to transcend all life experience. To assume the risks so knowingly and so willingly is to rise above all that is craven, sordid, limiting."

Civil rights attorney Martin Popper: "It must have come from a deeper source: an instinct for justice beyond that of most men, a greater sensitivity for the hurts of others, a stronger passion to set things right—or a blending of all these and other qualities which, when they were combined with a living curiosity and a knowledge of the world he lived in, added up to the making of a hero—the kind of hero who, because he responded to the call of the most oppressed of his fellows, gathered strength from them and, in so doing, moved the world. . . . It is sad that a cause needs dying for to make people understand its worth. But it is so. And if there were no one like Andy, life would not be worth living."

Algernon Black, leader of the American Ethical Movement: "They went down there trusting in America's promises; they trusted in the conscience of people; they weren't asking whether you were Jew, Catholic, or Protestant, Negro or White, Republican or Democrat, rich or poor; they were trusting the people of America to stand back of them as they went, unarmed, for the values they think made the world worth living in and without which they don't want to live and without which men have no respect; so there's a responsibility on every one of us and you can't walk out of it . . . So the question is not whether Andrew Goodman is dead; the question is whether we are dead or whether through his life and death we come alive."

When Andy was buried at the Mount Judah Cemetery in Queens, we weren't sure what to put on his tombstone. But then I heard about a poem written by Stephen Spender in 1933 called "I Think Continually of Those Who Were Truly Great." He wrote it to honor antifascists who had been killed by Franco in Spain, and he gave us permission to alter it slightly.

$\mathcal{A}$ndy and his companions became symbols of the intransigence of the South and the righteousness of the cause. Andy didn't go to Mississippi expecting to die. He simply went there to try to make it possible for people to go into a booth and vote. A hero? No. He was a beautiful, strong, determined person— and a great loss to his mother and father. He never aspired to martyrdom. But a martyr is what he became. Some of the seminal moments of the civil rights movement happened the year following his death, in 1965, including the historic march from Selma to Montgomery in Alabama and passage of the Voting Rights Act. They were inspired in no small part by the fate of three young men.

Two years after Andy's death, Bobby and I were inspired to carry on our son's goals and dreams. We started The Andrew Goodman Foundation, which supports projects that work to advance human rights, civil liberties, economic justice, and youth activism. The Foundation serves as a growing legacy to Andy Goodman, but he has been immortalized in many other ways. At Cornell, a stained glass window in Sage Chapel was designed and dedicated to honor Andy, Mickey, and James. At Queens College, the library is the site of the Chaney-Goodman-Schwerner Clock Tower. In front of the rebuilt Mount Zion Methodist Church in Mississippi stands a memorial to the three men "who gave their lives in the struggle to obtain human rights for all people." A four-block stretch of Manhattan's Upper West Side is named "Freedom Place" in their honor. Trevor Day School, at the location of the Walden School where all three of my sons attended, has named a building after Andy. Songs have been written about Andy, Mickey, and James by the likes of Pete Seeger and Simon and Garfunkel. There is even a 2,176-foot mountain overlooking Tupper Lake that has been christened Goodman Mountain.

But my favorite tribute to Andy came from a little girl. In the weeks following his death, I was so devastated that I could hardly get myself to read the hundreds upon hundreds of letters we received from well-wishers. But when I noticed that one letter had S.W.A.K. (Sealed With A Kiss) scrawled across the back of the envelope, I recognized it as the writing of a child. So I opened it.

"Dear Mr. and Mrs. Goodman," it began. "My name is Robin Goodman. I am ten years old, and I have a cat. Would you mind very much if I called him Andy?"

It was that kind of encounter—unexpected compassion and youthful innocence—that would remind me so much of my middle son, sending tears streaming down my cheeks.

Apparently, Robin had first seen Andy's picture in *The New York Times,* a black-and-white headshot that appeared endlessly (alongside those of Mickey and James) in newspapers across the nation. Robin noticed that she and Andy, though unrelated, shared a last name. Like Andy, she also had a father named Robert Goodman. And like Andy, her father had traveled south, from his home in New Jersey, to assist voter registration in Mississippi. More important (to a preteen girl), she thought Andy was just about the most handsome young man she had ever seen. She daydreamed about him constantly.

Robin went to camp that summer in upstate New York, where she and her friends watched the tragic story unfold over the next six weeks. Before the summer ended, the camp's cat delivered a litter of kittens, and a name-the-kitten contest was held. Robin noticed a tiny ball of black-and-white fur and instantly realized that it should be named Andy. His last name, she figured, should be Goodman, just like hers. And so it became.

When Robin returned to school that fall, she took up a collection to purchase two-way radios for civil rights workers, telling her classmates that this might have saved Andy and his friends. We continued to correspond occasionally. We invited her to Thanksgiving dinner, though she was unable to join us. As time passed and Robin became a teenager, we slowly fell out of touch.

The connections continued, however. Like Andy the thespian—and like my oldest son, Jonathan the musician—Robin pursued her dreams of becoming an artist. Like my youngest son, David, she attended Antioch College in Ohio. And like me, she eventually found herself married with two sons. Years later, in 1995, when her paintings were to appear at a gallery in the East Village, she sat down to make a list of people to invite. Her thoughts turned to me, whom she viewed as a woman who had reached out to a little girl despite my devastation. Of course, I interpreted it in much the opposite manner.

My friend Alie Fox joined me at the crowded gallery, and I told her that we should just stay for a moment. And after all, Robin had now reached middle age. I had no idea what she looked like. We took a look at Robin's wonderful art and prepared to leave. Then I heard a woman's voice. "Carolyn Goodman!"

I turned to see a curly-haired brunette. "I'm Robin Goodman."

And for the first time, we embraced—two women, neither of whom had been graced with a daughter, weeping in each other's arms, bonding over the memory of my son. Robin Goodman went on to become Robin Dash, an acclaimed artist and a member of the faculty at both Brandeis University and the

New England Conservatory. The cat, she later told me, lived for fifteen years with her family. They loved Andy Goodman, too.

THE EQUATION OF LIFE

All this knowledge, all this theoretical analysis
Children of the brain of man, so much
to know, so little understood and
we weary mortals stabbing here
jabbing there, enmeshed in the
net of it all.

I write poems for a week and then
spend the next week writing reports
on AC alternators—at the time realizing
no inconsistency, never the apparent
anomaly—the paradox of finite ways
and infinite needs. But comes the hour
of realization and questions, doubts,
despair, asked fondly sometimes,
cunningly at other times, persistently
always during the hour
What does it all mean? Where does it
all lead? Why the mystery to
life when death crowns it all
with oblivion or adds another
unknown to the equation of life?

—Bobby Goodman

SAVING MYSELF

$\mathcal{T}$he 1960s were a decade of tremendous loss to the country, particularly the deaths of the Kennedy brothers and Martin Luther King, Jr., and the casualties and pain of Vietnam. For many, the decade was one of distant but resounding horror, a sort of gradual destruction of ideals and the heralds of progressive change. For many, too, it was a personal horror—the loss of loved ones in distant jungles in a battle for dubious purposes. For me, the 1960s were a time of loss just as intimate but painfully random and relentless. I came close to losing myself in the pain, but I had learned years earlier that, in our times of greatest weakness, we can find strength we never knew we had.

I had discovered this years before, of course, during that difficult swim test at the summer camp on Echo Lake. But sometimes the test, as it were, simply appears too daunting. Sometimes you just want to drown.

Once when I was older, while swimming in the ocean I found myself caught in the tide. It was a public beach, and there were lifeguards on duty, but—let's face it—when it's a matter of life and death, survival is often up to you. So here I was, watching beachside buildings move by with terrifying speed as the current took hold of me. For a moment there I didn't think I was going to make it. But I gave it everything I had, trying mightily to free myself, this time with nobody to catch me if I went under. I survived that time, too—again, just barely.

It occurs to me that my "one arm over the other" mantra echoes a line from Emily Bronte's *Wuthering Heights*: "But you might as well bid a man struggling in the water, rest within arm's length of the shore! I must reach it first, and then I'll rest." As much as anything, that could serve as a metaphor for my journey through the decade.

The first test came when Bobby's father died in 1963. Charles Goodman and I had become very close. Bobby was always more like his mother, which is why I loved him. But I always sensed that I was more like his father. Charles was a fascinating man whose face had a lovely look about it. And he was a brilliant engineer. When he was younger, his hair was red, but supposedly it turned white while he was working as an assistant engineer for New York City's Board of Water Supply, overseeing construction of the Croton Reservoir, the largest public works water project in the world.

Eventually, Charles built his construction company, Grow Construction Corp., from the ground up. Grow was an acronym, actually. It stood for Goodman, Robert (Bobby, his eldest son), O'Henry (for Henry Jacoby, married to Bobby's sister Doris), and William (Bobby's brother Bill). The company owned a three-story building at 313 West Fifty-third Street and occupied offices on the top two floors. The bottom floor served as the alumni offices of Cooper Union, the city college which Charles had attended so many years earlier.

Among the thirteen children in his family, Charles was the only one who obtained a four-year college education—and only because Cooper Union is one of the few American institutions of higher learning to offer a full-tuition scholarship to all admitted students. He always considered his free education to be not only a springboard but also a reflection of the American Dream. So he became a dedicated alumnus. Indeed, one day in December 1963, only a couple of weeks after JFK's assassination, Charles was honored for his years of service on behalf of the school at a luncheon there. Afterward, he decided to walk back to his office.

Cooper Union is located at Seventh Street and Fourth Avenue. So here was an eighty-year-old man walking some fifty blocks uptown and nearly across town—a distance of almost three miles—on a cold December day. Typical Charles Goodman. When he finally arrived at Fifty-third Street and Eighth Avenue, he noticed a crew digging a foundation for what was going to be a multi-story municipal parking lot. The engineer on site was having some challenges because the foundation was very close to the Eighth Avenue subway. Charles had overseen construction of that subway some four decades earlier, so he decided to climb down a ladder into the trench and talk to the engineer. Again, typical Charles Goodman.

Eventually, he climbed out, walked to his office, and began to ascend the stairs. His heart gave out on the very top step. Obviously, it came as a terrible shock to all of us, although it does seem so appropriate that his last moments essentially encapsulated his journey: He started in a hole, made his way out of it, and went out on top.

Charles was full of life, so his death, as sudden as it was, was completely unexpected. But at least he had made it through eight decades. Twenty-year-old Andy's disappearance and death coming so soon after was obviously overwhelmingly traumatic. And the trauma was exacerbated by the subsequent trial.

Three days after Andy's body was discovered, we received a letter from President Johnson. He wrote, "Although no one can truly appreciate the utter desolation of parents who have lost a child—and particularly one just barely beginning adulthood— we are at least able to share some of the sorrow and grief. I am certain, however, that there must be some measure of comfort in the knowledge that your son, Andrew, lost his life in a cause that he believed in and which is truly significant in the affairs of mankind. I can assure you that the Federal Government's efforts to apprehend those who are responsible for this terrible crime will be intensified, and I am confident they will be found."

In December 1964, after a couple of Klansmen became FBI informants, nineteen men were, indeed, arrested for the crime: a motley crew of backwoods vigilantes—not only the sheriff and his deputy, but also a seventy-one-year-old Philadelphia cop, a seventeen-year-old high school dropout, and a Baptist preacher. None was tried for murder. The U.S. Justice Department reasoned that because murder was not a federal offense unless it was committed on federal property. The alternative was a state prosecution, but a state trial would have been a mockery at the time. Neither the state nor the county had conducted a serious investigation into the crime, and the would-be presiding judge was a white supremacist and even a distant cousin to at least one of the defendants. So instead, the Justice Department reached back to a Reconstruction-era statute and accused the defendants of depriving the victims of their civil rights.

In 1965, Judge William Harold Cox of the southern district of Mississippi threw the case out of court, only to be overruled by the U.S. Supreme Court. Finally, a year later and more than three years after the bodies were found, *United States v. Price, et al.* went to trial. By then, revoltingly, many of the defendants had become local folk heroes. Cecil Price was running for sheriff. The day after he was arrested, he remarked, "It took an hour to get to work this morning. I had to spend so much time shaking hands."

Eventually, eighteen Klansmen were indicted. When the verdicts were returned, only seven of the men (including Price, but not Sheriff Rainey) were found guilty. Only two of them received the maximum sentence. All were paroled early. None served more than six years in prison. Another eight men were acquitted, and three more trials resulted in deadlocked juries, including the trial of part-time preacher Edgar Ray Killen, who was said to have been a mastermind of the horror.

Remarkably, one juror admitted she just couldn't convict a man of God.

If I wasn't sure that I was going to survive the sorrow, I was even more concerned for Bobby. In the span of less than eight months, he lost his father and his son, and he may never have quite recovered. He never had what you would call robust health, the late 1930s tuberculosis episode being only the most signif-icant example. He had high blood pressure, and he took pills to control it. He was a rather excitable person, a worrier, and he put a great deal of pressure on himself, often unnecessarily.

By the late 1960s, Bobby was running the family business, a burden that fell on his shoulders as the oldest of Charles Goodman's five children and president of the company. But he was never really cut out for it. Sure, he was an excellent engineer, but he was a poet, first and foremost. He didn't have the disposition to run a company, particularly an undercapi-talized, high-risk company. He didn't have that DNA that a businessperson has to have, which includes a certain amount of detachment, a willingness to make decisions that could be tough on certain people. Bobby could never seem to fire anyone, for instance. He couldn't really talk sternly to them. He was a sweet man with a great deal of compassion. It makes for a wonderful husband and father. But as a businessperson, it often means that you find yourself surrounded by people of underwhelming competence, and the burden tends to boo-merang back up to the boss.

On top of it all, Bobby had taken it upon himself to run the nonprofit Pacifica Foundation, which was like a second full-time job. Pacifica Radio consists of independently operated, listener-supported, commercial-free radio stations around the country. It started in the late 1940s with a station in Berkeley, California (KPFA), but it eventually grew to include KPFK in Los Angeles, KPFT in Houston, WBAI in New York City, and WPFW in Washington, D.C., as well as dozens of affiliated stations. Part of its mission statement is to "engage in any activity that shall contribute to a lasting understanding between nations and between the individuals of all nations, races, creeds and colors; to gather and disseminate information on the causes of conflict between any and all of such groups; and through any and all means compatible with the purposes of this corporation to promote the study of political and economic problems and of the causes of religious, philosophical, and racial antagonisms."

Many of the people with whom Bobby worked at Pacifica might be described as well-intentioned but undisciplined, so he was forced to work hard. He was the kind of person who didn't do things partially. And delegating was not among his repertoire of talents. Between running Grow, Pacifica, and The Andrew Goodman Foundation, he was working eighty-hour weeks, although his fragile health dictated he should have been working half as long.

So here was my beloved Bobby, his health threatened by his intrinsic nature and his work ethic, his mind still reeling at the hate-spawned tragedy that had befallen the son who most resembled him, his soul burdened by his life experiences, his heart aching.

On one spring day in May 1969, Bobby went as usual to his office at West Fifty-third Street. Soon after, he complained of a headache and sat down. It worsened quickly, and Bobby's brother-in-law Henry took him to Mount Sinai Hospital. It turns out Bobby had suffered a stroke. I arrived as soon as I heard, spending the day there in that awful state of helplessness by a loved one's bedside. Watching the love of my life fade away seemed to drain my soul. By the evening, Bobby had lapsed into unconsciousness. When his younger sister Annette arrived, I had the sense that this was the new bedside shift. I was exhausted and confused by a troubling lack of communication with the doctors about Bobby's condition and his prognosis, but essentially they told me: *Go home. Come back in the morning. He'll be fine until then.* To my lasting regret, that's what I did.

Annette stayed there all night, talking to her brother periodically, hoping he could hear her. And then, in the wee hours of the morning, perhaps at four or five o'clock, she heard a groan from Bobby's direction. She ran into the room, and the nurse told her Bobby had just died. He was three months shy of his fifty-fifth birthday. And I wasn't there to hold his hand while he took his last breath.

Carolyn and Bobby, 1960

Bobby had never truly come to terms with Andy's death. Certainly, none of us really had. But Bobby in particular was less disposed to detachment, to moving on by keeping busy. He had a sweater that had belonged to Andy, for instance, and he wore it all the time. So although it was a brain hemorrhage that killed him, I suspect that the weight of so much grief was something he couldn't survive.

Within five years, I lost my son and my husband, both very much in the prime of their lives. What now? Bobby and I used to attend concerts of the New York Philharmonic at Lincoln Center. Several acquaintances who had sat behind us for many years, upon hearing of Bobby's death, lamented gently and anecdotally that he had been their barometer of judgment regarding the symphony's performance. When they saw Bobby clapping wildly in front of them with a rapturous expression on his face, well, then they knew that they had just listened to something superb. How, they wondered, will we know what's magnificent?

Music, so often my respite from the world's troubles, became an outlet for finally letting go of all my emotions regarding my losses. But it didn't happen immediately. It happened later, while I was visiting Israel and listening to a concert at an open-air coliseum. Suddenly, in an ancient land, beneath a cloudless sky, while world-class musicians brought to life the painstakingly crafted composition of a musical genius, I began to sob uncontrollably. *Bobby is gone. How will I know what is magnificent?*

On Bobby's gravestone, I had three words engraved: "POET—HUMANIST—ENGINEER." Just his name, the years of his birth and death, and those three words. He was a man who built bridges, in every sense, and he was a bridge to sanity in my life. When I lost him, following closely the loss of my surrogate father and my beautiful son, I fell into a deep depression, so deep that I wasn't sure I had the strength to swim to the surface. At Bobby's memorial service, a friend approached me and told me that my strength, which she so admired, would carry me on.

"My strength," I told her, "just died."

$\mathcal{I}$ was still in my early fifties. My surviving sons had left the nest. My husband was gone. And in many ways, I had spent years defining myself by the men in my life. I had obviously reached a critical juncture, and I came to an equally critical realization: I always felt I couldn't live my life as if it all but stopped on that fateful day in 1964 when Andy went missing because if I did, my son's death wouldn't have any lasting significance. Likewise, if I let the loss of my beloved Bobby reduce my sense of self, then I would lose significance, too. Fortunately, once again I had underestimated my will to survive, to nurture and keep alive this flame of passion, this zest for living, which all the men in my world had given me. I had to forge a life on my own. I had to keep my head above water. And that's what I did.

Not long before Bobby died, after nearly a decade of stops and starts toward my advanced education, I received my doctorate in education from Columbia University Teacher's College, and I found practical ways to integrate my activism and my profession—by becoming involved in community psychology. I became an assistant clinical professor of psychiatry at Albert Einstein College of Medicine, and at the Bronx Psychiatric Center I inaugurated the Parent and Child Education (PACE) program, which was designed for emotionally disturbed mothers with high-risk preschool children. Equally important, I convinced the State of New York to fund it.

PACE filled a void in the burgeoning concept of community mental health. When a mother suffers from mental or emotional disorders, or from drug and alcohol addiction, or from memories of childhood neglect and abuse, what happens to her own children? At best, it is not easy to be a parent. Given a cluster of psychosocial problems, plus economic difficulties, children of such parents are especially vulnerable to emotional, behavioral, and learning disorders. PACE was an attempt to stop the pain and deprivation of one generation from carrying over to the next. The staff consultants, students, and volunteers at PACE became the "family" where an isolated, disturbed patient could find her identity as a woman and mother. Caring for mother and child together in a non-institutional setting that fostered trust, we started with twenty mothers and two dozen children. Within a decade, we recorded more than five thousand annual visits.

The program brought the children to the hospital so that they could spend time with their mothers. Meanwhile, trained counselors taught the mothers healthier ways to interact with the children—to help them understand child development and how important it was to offer their children love and tolerance. Only twelve years later, the Board of Hospital and Community Psychiatry of the American Psychiatric Association honored me with its Gold Award for program excellence as a reflection of the PACE Family Treatment Center's success. PACE was also the recipient of the Ruth Kirzon Group Humanitarian Award for

Services to Handicapped Children. Of course, the real reflection of success was in the faces of the women and children who benefited from it.

I never approached the women in the PACE program as patients. They were mothers. That's what we called them. We wanted to foster a sense of intimacy and trust, but still on occasion we had to overcome great distances. One woman in particular was one of the most difficult mothers in the program. She was highly intelligent, but she had been abused and neglected as a child, and the same pattern was beginning to show in her behavior toward her daughters. Essentially, she had no tolerance for children at all. And she seemed to have no use for me either. This woman believed I had no concept of what real pain was, of what it means to suffer. She pegged me as a rich bitch, slumming it occasionally on a charitable whim. Until one day, when she was looking away from me and staring at the bookcases in my office, she noticed a memorial book for Andy on one of the shelves.

"Andrew Goodman," she said, quite out of the blue. "Was he a relative of yours?"

I nodded. "He was my son."

And it was as if the floodgates had opened. She broke down and cried. She stood up and hugged me. Suddenly, we were no longer adversaries who seemed to come from different planets; we were friends, connected through an understanding of pain and loss. And we remained friends, long after she began responding to our efforts, turning herself into a success story. Many years later, when a local newscast reported that I had been arrested during a protest, she called me to tell me how worried she had been when she heard the news. She was now nurturing and empathetic—mothering, you might say.

In some ways, I believe social justice and psychology are one and the same. After all, both are more than abstract concepts; they are about individual people. Everyone has equal value and should have equal opportunity. So my pursuit of social justice didn't wane; indeed, I grew busier than ever.

In 1972 I was elected chairperson of The Pacifica Foundation Board, a role Bobby had played. He had purchased a deconsecrated church on East Sixty-second Street in New York, which was to be renovated and converted into a studio for WBAI. I continued his efforts by spearheading a campaign to raise funds for the capital acquisition costs. During my tenure as chairperson, we were able to launch KPFW in D.C. and also put KPFT back on the air in Houston after some dramatic and frightening events.

On May 12, 1970, just two months after going on the air, the station's transmitter had been bombed. Nearly five months later, on October 6 (which happened to be my fifty-fifth birthday), the transmitter was bombed yet again while the station was broadcasting Arlo Guthrie's "Alice's Restaurant." This time, the damage was significantly more extensive. After months of inactivity by the FBI and Houston police, Pacifica took the initiative to mount a media campaign designed to draw attention to the unsolved case and pressure authorities to act. Ultimately, federal agents arrested a member of the Ku Klux Klan and charged him with the bombings, as well as with plotting to blow up the Pacifica radio stations in Berkeley and Los Angeles. He was convicted and imprisoned—yet another awful encounter, albeit indirectly, that I had with the hateful KKK.

During the 1970s, I also became active in the Givat Haviva Educational Foundation in New York City and the Givat Haviva Institute, which supports activists who work to advance Jewish-Arab relations in Israel. Founded by the Kibbutz Artzi Movement, a federation of eighty-three kibbutzim throughout Israel, the Institute has been educating for peace, democracy, coexistence, and social solidarity since 1949.

In 1976, Rabbi Bruce Cohen, affiliated with Givat Haviva, approached me to help him found Interns for Peace (IFP). I became chairperson in the mid-1980s and remained on the board until 2000. IFP began in Israel in 1976 and expanded into the Palestinian West Bank and Gaza, Africa, Europe, and the United States. The program trained ethnic community peace workers to unite their conflicting peoples in cooperative, inter-communal activities to build bridges of understanding. More than two hundred peace workers engaged tens of thousands of Jews and Arabs in business, cultural, educational, athletic, and community development projects. It might be said that the goal, in many cases, was to convince people—especially young people—that tolerance is an alternative to terror. Many of these interns/peace workers became lifelong advocates for coexistence and sometimes full-time professionals. It was a grassroots approach to social change, which obviously appealed to me.

One of the founders of Givat Haviva was a man named Menachem Bader, who became my close friend. His story personifies the notion that acts of kindness and reconciliation can save us. Born in Austria-Hungary, he emigrated to Germany with his family. He graduated from the University of Cologne and then moved to pre-State Israel in the 1920s. During World War II, Menachem was an emissary of the "Rescue Committee" of the Jewish community. He became a member of the first Israeli Knesset in 1949 and eventually general director of Israel's Ministry of Development.

In the 1930s, Menachem founded a kibbutz right next to an Arab village. Back then, the Arabs, who were generally poor, would come in at night and steal livestock and supplies, thinking the kibbutz had plenty of wealth, which it didn't. Menachem wanted to stop that, so he got the men in the kibbutz to take their shovels, put them over their shoulders and march under the midday sun, so that from far away the sun would reflect off the steel, and the Arabs would be intimidated by what seemed like armed strength. The thefts stopped, but Menachem didn't. He wanted more than just uneasy peace; he wanted harmony. So he decided to attach a white flag to a pole and march into the Arab village. Soon the villagers and the kibbutzniks were friends.

One Arab villager asked Menachem for a favor. The man's son collected stamps, so the man asked Menachem, who traveled all over the world, if he would save the stamps on his letters and give them to his son. And Menachem did. A few years later, by which time many Arabs had been brought to Europe as servants, Menachem was in Germany rescuing Jews and bringing them to Palestine via what was essentially an underground railroad. His scheme was quite successful for some time, but this time he was captured.

Menachem figured the jig was up. But one day, as he sat on his bed in his jail cell, the door opened. In came an orderly bringing him something to eat. And who was the orderly? The Arab from the next village, the one whose son collected stamps. He helped Menachem escape—a good man helping a great man complete his righteous duties. The moral of the story is that creative ways of reconciling, of making peace even when it seems so distant and unlikely do exist. And we are all saved by such practices. I saw the same optimism and persistence in the brave men and women who risked all by trying to foster racial harmony in the Deep South. They weren't down there to be "outside agita-tors." They were simply seeking a way for people to live together. Of course, I continued the search myself. I took part in antiwar demonstrations, marched in civil rights rallies, and told my story to countless religious and student groups. I spoke at churches and synagogues and museums, at the Civil Rights Memorial in Montgomery, at the United Nations, and at dozens of schools and universities—from Harvard to Yeshiva to Queens College, where I received the President's Award at the graduation cere-mony, a ceremony Andy had never been able to attend.

Indeed, I was flattered to receive many honors and awards over the years, including the Heschel-King Award for Interfaith Activism presented by the Temple of Universal Judaism and the Park Avenue Christian Church and the Civil Rights Leadership Award, presented to me at the Embassy of Israel in Washington, D.C. More than being honored, however, I was grateful because such ceremonies gave me an opportunity to spread my mes-sage—that today's activists are following in the footsteps of a long line of passionate people, that by bettering the world they are standing on the shoulders of giants. Indeed, I would always tell people that I had been very lucky. "Lucky?" they would reply. "How can you say that after suffering so many losses?" I would explain that my losses have given me strength because they are a legacy for young people, who can envision that risks are worth-while when the goal is to create a peaceful and just world.

To my surprise, I even began to find a measure of personal healing, as the days became weeks and the weeks became months and years. When Bobby died, I remember telling people close to me that I would never get married again. And I fully expected that to be the case. Bobby was the kind of love that comes around once in a lifetime if you're lucky. I went out with many people. I was still relatively young and had lots of friends. But nothing really excited me about any of the men I met.

Then one day, a friend of mine invited me over for dinner. "I have a friend visiting from California," she said, "and I thought you might like to go out with him. I have a boyfriend, and the four of us can go to the theater."

When I walked into her house, I recognized her boyfriend as a man named Joe Eisner. I had known him before. He and his former wife had attended a party or two at our apartment. His family owned New York Gas Lighting Company, a wholesale and retail lighting fixtures business in the Bowery district, which Joe's father had started way back in 1911. We had once purchased a light fixture from Joe, but I certainly didn't know him well. That night, however, something happened. We looked at each other, and there was a spark. We both felt it at the time. Looking back, I could see that it was not unlike that first spark with Bobby, only back then I was the one who had a significant other on my arm. I don't know why that is. Attraction is impossible to explain.

A couple of weeks later, I had tickets to a concert. The person with whom I was supposed to go had become ill. So I decided to take a chance. I called Joe Eisner. He was free—my friend thought he was still her boyfriend; I don't know that Joe felt the same. We listened to the music together that evening, and, well, the melodies that began that night were to resonate long after. We were married in 1972.

Carolyn and Joe, 1972

Joe was a native New Yorker. For many years, he and his parents and three older siblings lived in an apartment in Lower Manhattan, only a block away from the lighting store in the Bowery. From there, he went to North Carolina State University as the only member of his family to attend college. A history major, he intended for a while to go into teaching, but he ended up succumbing to the lure of the family business. He married a woman named Helen Geller, who came from a successful

family. Her father, Andrew Geller, had started out as a shoe ped-
dler. Over the years, his efforts resulted in a multimillion-dollar
shoe company that still bears his name. Helen was an impressive
woman—a Phi Beta Kappa at Smith College, where she was an
actress, an editor of the newspaper, a member of the basketball
team. She and Joe had a family of four boys to raise on the Lower
East Side, so Joe remained a fixture in lighting fixtures, sticking
with the business until his death.

Joe and I had much in common. We had both lost our
spouses in the late 1960s (Helen succumbed to breast cancer
right about the time of Bobby's death). We had each raised a
brood of boys. We shared a dry wit. Joe knew how to deliver
a one-liner, and he always seemed to have a reservoir of them.
And we were on the same page politically, although I was admittedly far more vocal about it. In fact, he was decidedly uncontro-
versial. He was a tremendous intellectual, and he had his opin-
ions, but he rarely expressed them unless someone else raised
the issue first. So perhaps we were the perfect complement to
each other.

Like many wives, I suppose I set the tone in the relationship, especially socially. I orchestrated the comings and goings
on Eighty-sixth Street where Joe and I lived, raising money for
this program or that movement. And I entertained guests at
the small house Joe owned in upstate Putnam County, a country respite with a stream running along the ten-acre property.

Joe would just go along for the ride—unless he didn't want to, in which case he would basically go on strike. He was as reclusive and reticent and introverted as I wasn't. I loved to hold court—in fact, someone once described me as a sort of Gertrude Stein of the Upper West Side. Joe seemed to enjoy it at times, as well, but often he would prefer to simply curl up with a good philosophy book.

My second husband was a fine painter, though he never gave it quite the time that he could have. He might have been excellent, perhaps even making a living that way. But just about all of Joe's still life paintings and portraits—several of which we hung in the apartment—were created during private classes he took with renowned expressionist painter Joseph Solman. Joe rarely painted outside of classroom situations, although he was finally convinced to have a showing at a small gallery. I loved going to art museums with him, though, because he had an eye for art that was well beyond mine. He saw things and knew things that could turn my experience of any piece of artwork into a beautiful reverie. Joe unleashed the wonders of art for me the same way Bobby had done it for music and poetry.

We traveled extensively together around the world—that is, when I could get Joe to go, too. I don't think he was crazy about it, but I guess he was crazy enough about me to come along. So we went to the Caribbean and to Puerto Rico nearly every year, chartering a private sailboat. We went to France and Italy and

Greece. Close to home, we traveled with friends aboard a barge on the Erie Canal, going from one end to the other through all the locks and such, learning history along the way.

Still, Joe and I gave each other a fair amount of space, which is probably something we both needed at the time, having met in midlife, which is a bit like climbing aboard a moving train. He needed someone like me to bring some social stimulation and energy into his world. I treasured him for the intellectual stimulation he gave me. That and the long leash.

The union lasted nearly two decades, until Joe's death in 1992. Once again, it happened in an instant. We were in the apartment, and Joe, who had experienced some heart problems before, told me he was having chest pains. I laid him down on the bed and dialed 911. Then I saw the look on his face, and I knew that he was going to die then and there. It was yet another sudden loss of a great man in my life. But during those years with Joe I had regained something vital—my resolve.

JUSTICE

$\mathcal{I}$n 1989, I finally went to Mississippi. It seems incredible that during all the years in which the state had played such a large part in my life, I had never traveled there. I had never actually walked in the places where these terrible events—Andy's arrest, his incarceration, his murder—had taken place. I decided it was time to come face to face with my demons, so I decided to recognize the silver anniversary of the tragedy by forming a coalition of the families of the victims, leading a Freedom Caravan into the South and educating a new generation about old injustices. James Chaney's younger brother Ben joined us. We showed civil rights films, held panel discussions, visited schools and libraries. The Freedom Caravan was scheduled to wind its way north to New York City. It started in Philadelphia, that Mississippi hamlet that had long been such a dark place to me. As we rode a bus along the same route, the same highway tragically traversed by my son, chills ran down my spine. I was reliving the experience. It is nearly impossible to articulate the emotion, but I was there with them. It was a cathartic experience, and perhaps a long overdue one.

Twenty-five years after the horrors of 1964, Philadelphia was a quarter century distant from the stories that I had been told. People still stared at outsiders, but I sensed they were more curious than contemptuous. A monument to the Confederacy stood in front of the Neshoba County Courthouse, but it seemed more a historical relic than a statement of allegiance. There remained a predominantly white part of town and a predominantly black part of town, but daily encounters suggested a more integrated environment. Indeed, I was stunned by the fact that the Secretary of State of Mississippi—a man named Dick Molpus, who was born in Philadelphia—actually rose in front of a large gathering and apologized for the events of the 1960s. I couldn't believe my ears. The moment was so profound for me, so therapeutic. Afterward, I walked across the stage, and the two of us just held each other. "If you ever had a moment where you immediately connected with someone, that happened to me in that second," he later explained. "We became a part of each other's lives."

Of course, as William Faulkner wrote about his native Mississippi, "The past is never dead. It's not even past." There were still whispers about a vibrant underground Ku Klux Klan and black men dying while in police custody. There were still African-American folks in the area who had never voted in their lives. And there were still a few residents, some of them even passing as respected citizens, who had been among the monsters arrested for my son's murder.

Did I consider confronting the perpetrators of my nightmares? Not for a second. I never wanted any part of them in my life. I didn't want to see them nor connect myself with them in any way. I had learned a great deal about myself in confronting my hatred of those men—hatred so intense that it was beyond intellectual; it was almost physical—and about the need to maintain my faith in humanity, despite being victimized by inhumanity. I knew those men were there and that there were others like them. But my mission was to reach out to the wonderful people of Mississippi, who are there in great numbers, too. I wanted to find the people who wished to fight evil, not the people who perpetuate it.

When the 1989 Freedom Caravan pulled out of Philadelphia, I feared it would fail, that people wouldn't want to immerse themselves in the agonies of the past to ward off the hazards of the future. I worried that when the caravan finally arrived at its terminus at New York's Cathedral of St. John the Divine the church would be filled only with echoes. But the caravan added a bus here, a car there, a van, a motorcycle, a convoy of supporters. When we finally arrived at the cathedral, we were met by a beautiful sight—a line of people around the block, hoping to get in. I took it as a sign and a calling. People want to know. *They want to know.*

Five years later, I decided to organize Freedom Summer '94 under the auspices of The Andrew Goodman Foundation. We aimed to provide training and technical assistance to young people all over the country who were hoping to turn social conscience into action—the Andy Goodmans and James Chaneys and Mickey Schwerners of the 1990s. At the center-piece of the summer, a trio of workshops would bring young activists together—one in Cleveland, one in Seattle, and in per-haps the ultimate full-circle tribute to my martyred son, one in Philadelphia, Mississippi.

Incidentally, I learned something else: A tiny hamlet of per-haps one hundred residents lies right on the outskirts of the city of Philadelphia. It is called Hope.

We tend to look at transcendental figures, usually those peo-ple whose feats exemplify the dreams and priorities of the era, and call them "heroes." For me as a child, one such hero was Charles Lindbergh, who flew solo over the Atlantic from New York to Paris in 1927. I had no way of knowing that we would later share the pain of losing a son amid national headlines. At the time, we just shared an imagination.

One day, as I was supposed to be staying after school for help in arithmetic, I heard that Lindbergh was to be featured in the RKO newsreel at the local movie house. When you're eleven, and you're given a choice between long division and a date with a hero, there is no choice. So I left. I wasn't playing hooky, exactly. I just wasn't staying after school with Cedarhurst Grammar School's eighth-grade teacher, Mrs. Hazel Hicks— who happened to see me leave because I walked right past the classroom window en route to my rendezvous with my idol. I still remember the withering glare she gave me and the trouble I caught after she told my mother. But I got to see Charles Lindbergh, bigger than life on the big screen. Small rebellions can lead to small victories.

Only much later did I learn of Lindbergh's anti-Semitism, discovering that my onetime hero was all too flawed. I learned, too, over the years, that heroism is not a matter of traveling beyond the traditional limits of human experience; it's about immersing oneself within the human experience. It means standing for principle, risking for a cause, righting wrongs.

Some seven decades after I crept to the theater to catch a glimpse of Lindbergh, I produced a documentary film about true heroes. It was an attempt to debunk the national myth— perpetuated by the national media so intent on portraying modern youth as cynical, apathetic, even nihilistic—that young people had abandoned the activist legacy of their parents. Quite the

contrary, I discovered young organizers addressing issues rang-
ing from education and ecology to voter registration and racial
tension.

Interspersed with archival footage and the wisdom of those
who have gone before them in this nation's long tradition of
youth activism, the documentary took us around the country
to see what young people with passion were doing. People like
Miya Yoshitani, a University of North Carolina student who
led the Student Environmental Action Coalition, and Emily
Barcklow, founder of a youth-led, adult-supported organization
called the Seattle Young People's Project.

I called the documentary *Hidden Heroes,* and the concept
has become a focus of The Andrew Goodman Foundation's
Hidden Heroes Program, which aims to inspire, educate, and
honor those who take responsibility for healing the world. The
goal is to recognize the young people out there who have discovered that empathy is empowering, a notion that harkens back to
my Lindbergh epiphany: You simply can't make a difference in
other people's lives if you are determined to fly solo.

A few years later, the Foundation began working with a
group of independent directors to produce another documentary film, called *Neshoba,* named after the county where Andy's
life was stolen from him. It started with the purpose of assuring
that the fortieth anniversary of his death would not pass unno-
ticed, but it soon became much more—an examination of the

climate of attitudes, both changed and unchanged, surrounding a new trial about an old injustice. You see, over those four
decades, a groundswell had been building, a search for justice
continued by many of the people who became the true heroes
in my life.

People like the wonderful Stanley Dearman, who spent
34 years as the editor of the *Neshoba Democrat,* taking over a
newspaper whose previous editor had declared two months
before the murders, "Outsiders who come in here and try to stir
up trouble should be dealt with in a manner they won't forget."
Stanley, a native of Meridian, became a courageous and progressive voice of reason and a good friend. While he decried
media depictions of "a bunch of rednecks standing in tight little
knots on the streets of Philadelphia," he courageously detailed
the extent and menace of the Ku Klux Klan's involvement in
the murders and its continuing threat to the good people of
Mississippi. Even more than three decades later, after he had
finally sold the newspaper, Stanley told one interviewer, "The
Klan, people of that mentality are still around. Quite a few, I'd
guess. A lot of them are ready to shoot me now. I'm not scared
of them. I never was scared of them."

People, too, like the intrepid Jerry Mitchell, who has
won so many awards for his journalism and for his relentless quest to bring unpunished killers to justice that one colleague once described him as "the South's Simon Wiesenthal."

An investigative reporter for *The Clarion-Ledger* in Jackson, Mississippi, Jerry was inspired to look into cold civil rights cases after watching the movie *Mississippi Burning*. His dogged work contributed to putting several Klansmen behind bars, including Byron De La Beckwith (for the assassination of Medgar Evers), Sam Bowers (for the murder of Vernon Dahmer) and Bobby Cherry (for the Birmingham church bombings). Sometimes, he simply looked where no one else had bothered to look. For instance, Cherry's alibi had been that he was watching wrestling on TV when the bomb was planted inside the church. Mitchell checked old TV schedules and discovered no wrestling program had been on at the time.

People like Allison Nichols, Brittany Saltiel, and Sarah Siegel—three students from Adlai Stevenson High School in Lincolnshire, Illinois. The girls, with the help of their inspiring teacher Barry Bradford, turned a National History Day assignment into an award-winning ten-minute documentary and a crusade to get the "Mississippi Burning" case reopened. They worked with Mississippi citizens, law enforcement officials, civil rights movement veterans, and the media. The documentary won a school prize, but it also prompted a group of congressmen to ask officials to reopen the investigation. For their efforts, Allison, Brittany, and Sarah earned recognition on the floor of the U.S. Congress by the likes of Senator Barack Obama, and they forever earned my gratitude, not only for their accomplishments but for their roles as shining examples that youth activism is alive and well in America.

People like Dick Molpus, whose apology as Mississippi Secretary of State did much to galvanize efforts for justice and who pushed for a multiracial movement to address the reality of racism in the region. And Susan Glisson, Director of the William Winter Institute for Racial Reconciliation, who made that real by formally organizing the Philadelphia Coalition, an integrated group of citizens (blacks, whites, Choctaws) who pushed for indictment of Edgar Ray Killen, the Klan leader who had been roaming free for several decades despite having coordinated the killings of my son and his companions.

Those are the real heroes—people who wouldn't let go. Some risked their livelihood and even their lives to stand up to hate groups, to pursue the truth, to agitate for justice. In fact, I would say they became some of the most important people in my life.

$\mathcal{I}$n 1999, Mississippi Attorney General Mike Moore reexamined and reopened the then thirty-five-year-old case against Edgar Ray Killen, with the state contemplating murder charges for the first time. Two years later, Deputy Cecil Price, who was likely to testify, died after falling from a lift in an equipment rental store in Philadelphia, a development that was considered a blow to the case. More than a few people suspected it was no accident. But the momentum generated by the aforementioned heroes was enough to bring it to a grand jury in 2004 (by then, the state attorney general was Jim Hood). A phone call to me from Jerry Mitchell in January 2005 brought news of Killen's arrest. The state was, indeed, charging him with murder.

So once again, I returned to Philadelphia, Mississippi. But this time, I didn't do so to further the cause of tolerance and lend my voice to a brighter future. This time, I was going to be asked to relive the past.

James Chaney's mother, Fannie Lee, was there. And his brother Ben. And Rita Bender, who had been Mickey Schwerner's wife. My son David accompanied me to the trial. In fact, I seemed to be shadowed the whole four days I was down there. One of the officials told David, "I'm going to get you and your mother a driver, and he's going to be with you wherever you go—and I do mean wherever you go." Sure enough, during the trial, I told the man assigned to us that I needed to go to the bathroom. I figured he would simply point me in the right direction. But no, he accompanied me right to the door and stood guard the whole time I was in there. Later, when we were boarding the airplane to leave and I commented that it was a relief to be going home, David explained to me that the man was actually a bodyguard. "That man was on the lookout," he said, "because they had been told that the Klan is still out to get you."

At the trial itself, I took the stand, and I was asked to identify a picture of Andy, who always looked so dreamy-eyed yet
so alive. Then they asked me to read the postcard Andy had
sent upon arriving in Mississippi, the one from my mantelpiece. By the time I gathered myself, started reading, and somehow made it through the task—by the time, that is, that I said
the words "All my love, Andy"—I'm not sure there was a dry
eye in the courtroom.

Carolyn on the witness stand, 2005

Well, except for Killen, who just sat there expressionless.
I never saw him show any emotion. He never apologized, of
course. Sitting amid the spectators, I found my eyes drawn to
the man, who was confined to a wheelchair after breaking his
legs in a logging accident. I just had to look at him, and believe
me, he wasn't an easy man to look at. I wondered, *What goes
through that man's head?*

As Dr. King once put it, "Injustice anywhere is a threat to justice everywhere." That's really all I wanted—justice. Not vengeance. Not death for the man who masterminded the killing of my son. I always was against capital punishment and remained so, despite being intimately familiar with the kind of personal tragedy that is said to test such notions. Ending Edgar Ray Killen's life wouldn't solve anything. How would it help?

When the verdict was returned, the jury acquitted Killen of murder. But this time, he was convicted of three counts of manslaughter. The verdict came down on June 21, 2005, exactly forty-one years to the day after he and the Klan murdered Andy, Mickey, and James. The judge ordered that he receive a twenty-year sentence for each count and that the sentences be served consecutively, meaning eighty-year-old Edgar Ray Killen was sure to die behind bars.

I felt relief, not only because I had long envisioned locking up this monster, but also because I had long hoped for the sense of closure that it might give to so many people who had been victims of the Klan. And there were many. A display at the Civil Rights Memorial in Montgomery includes the names of men and women who died in the 1950s and 1960s under circumstances suggesting they were victims of racially motivated violence. Have you ever heard of Isadore Banks? His charred corpse was found chained to a tree in Arkansas in 1954. Mattie Green? A bomb exploded under her house in Georgia in 1960.

James Earl Motley? He died in an Alabama jail in 1967 after suffering three severe blows to the head from a deputy sheriff. More than seventy other names are listed.

So the observers in the courtroom included wives and husbands and siblings and cousins of the Klan's victims, many of whom were about my age. They came from all over the country, and they could finally feel as if justice had been served.

Perhaps the most profound element of the experience, however, was the simple juxtaposition between what the judge said in 2005 and what another judge had said thirty-eight years earlier. In 1967, following the weak sentencing of only a handful of the killers, Judge Cox had made this inexcusable and inaccurate statement: "They killed one nigger, one Jew, and one white man. I gave them all what I thought they deserved."

Thirty-eight years later, Judge Marcus Gordon's post-sentencing statement included this observation: "I have taken into consideration that there are three lives involved in this case, and the three lives should absolutely be respected."

FLING STARS

To Jonathan, Andrew and David,

Take time—my sons—make time
That its bloom will always be—
Each day is but a moment's pause
In the ineffable rush of eternity.

Make fire—my sons—take fire
That your flame will always glow
Let day become a vagrant sun
In the ever ebb of its silent flow.

Take peace—my sons—make peace
With the spin of the soil and sea
Fling stars—my sons—bring stars
My sons—And sing my sons—with ecstasy.

—Bobby Goodman

NO TWILIGHT

$\mathcal{S}$ix years before those verdicts brought a measure of justice, I was arrested at the age of eighty-three. I had been protesting the killing of Guinean immigrant Amadou Diallo. He had been shot to death after four New York City cops, approaching his building while searching for a rapist, thought he reached for a gun. They shot at him forty-one times, pumping nineteen bullets into him. As it turned out, he was unarmed.

I was not alone in my anger. More than two hundred people were arrested in front of the New York City police headquarters on that spring day, and hundreds more were taken into custody over a two-week span, including people like former New York City Mayor David Dinkins, Congressman Charles Rangel, playwright Tony Kushner, actress Susan Sarandon, and comedian

Dick Gregory. But I suppose my arrest received particular attention, given my age and my son Andy's martyrdom. "We have just lived through another murder of another man," I told the media, and I meant it. However, throughout the whole process I was thinking less of Andy's death than Andy's courage.

When an organizer of the protests had called me to ask me if I would be willing to risk being arrested by standing in front of the police headquarters, I thought about how my son volunteered to travel to an unfamiliar and unwelcoming land in an attempt to register a disenfranchised portion of its population. He was supposed to go to a less dangerous place in Mississippi, but when the church burned near Philadelphia he had told me on the phone, "Mom, I want to go where it will make a difference. I might get arrested, but it's important." I thought, *If he was willing to risk it on the dirt roads of Mississippi, surely I can stand up for my beliefs on the streets of my hometown.*

So I stood at the front door of the police headquarters, along with more than a dozen other older women. The policemen asked us to move. We didn't. So they arrested us, charging us with disorderly conduct. It wasn't the first time I had been arrested (I protested Nelson Mandela's continued jailing in 1990), and I knew it was primarily a matter of going through the motions. The cops were friendly enough, helping us old ladies into the police vehicle and placing us in plastic handcuffs that were so loose we could free ourselves at any time. They asked us a bunch of questions when we arrived at the precinct and then chatted us up as they watched to make sure we didn't escape. Given the median age of our group, it would have been the slowest escape in the history of jailbreaks. Not much of a physical or emotional sacrifice. To be honest, my biggest worry as we sat in the jail cell for eight hours without food was whether I would be released in time to make use of my theater tickets that night. Still, I was proud of myself, at my age, for being part of the protest, for continuing to perpetuate Andy's legacy by taking action when I saw a need for it.

My son, David, often told a story about that day. A colleague of his ran into his office, telling him that he had just seen his mother on television—being carted off to jail.

"Well," David shrugged, "that happens from time to time."

As we waited at the police precinct, I watched a group of mostly minority prisoners being placed in holding cells before being shuffled off to somewhere or another. The doors to the cells were closed with a chilling clang, and the prisoners just sat there, waiting for whatever was going to happen to them. That might serve as a representation of aging—or at least for the way I vowed not to live the so-called twilight of my life.

I was lucky to live a long life and a satisfying one. How many people can say that? I did most of the things I wanted to do. But that didn't mean I would be satisfied with stagnation. So many elderly people don't know what to do with themselves. Time hangs heavy. But that was not the case with me. Never. I kept pushing. I kept learning. Indeed, by the time I reached my nineties, I had learned a great many things.

I learned that life is too short for small talk. I never had much patience for it. *Where did you eat last night? How was the food? Do you have a good recipe?* I couldn't stand it. I would shut up like a clam. People may have thought I was arrogant, but it just didn't interest me. It reminded me of a line from "The Love Song of J. Alfred Prufrock" by T.S. Eliot, in which he examines, through the introspections of the narrator, the emptiness and soulless quality of the bleak social world surrounding him: *In the room, the women come and go / Talking of Michelangelo . . .*

Then again, I could understand the benefit of using small talk when approaching a new acquaintance. Even in my later years, I would attend a concert and then ride home alone on a bus late at night. People told me I was crazy to do that at my age, but this was my city, and I was well aware of where and when I could be on my own. I would make my way onto the bus and see someone sitting nearby. Often, the person would be staring into space, looking depressed, perhaps even unfriendly. And I would see it as a challenge. I would say something banal like, "Boy, the bus sure is crowded for this hour"— something that gently called for a response, just to see where it would lead. Again, my curiosity about people informed my actions. And I realized that the best way to gain entrance to people's souls is to let people talk. People love to be listened to. So it was small talk as a means to an end, but please, not as an end itself.

I learned that I could do more than I ever thought I could and that perhaps I should expect less of others. I always set the bar high for people with whom I worked on various projects, and at times I would have a pretty short fuse. In fact, I could get downright angry. But I like to think that—ironically, while working toward tolerance in the big picture—I finally began to grow tolerant of other people's flaws and failings.

Also, I found that my instincts about people were usually right. I felt I had a sense of such things, and I have met so many dedicated and inspiring people amid my various projects and pursuits. Usually, I could sense this rather immediately. Eli Lee, my friend and colleague for several years with The Andrew Goodman Foundation, noticed this when we first met in 1989. As a student at Columbia, he called me out of the blue one day to say he would like to work for me. I told him to come on over to the apartment. When I answered the door, I said simply, "Hi, Eli. I'm Carolyn. Here's one hundred dollars. Will you go buy some stamps? We have to get a mailing out." Eli would say, upon retelling the story, "She knew me for about seventeen seconds, and she gave me one hundred dollars!" But trust can be an instinct. When I knew, I knew. And besides, his cold call to me signaled his compassion.

I learned that getting old is a matter of course but also a case of mind over matter. As I aged, one of the most painful things to me was not only seeing my peers pass away but also seeing them deteriorate. When I noticed decline in my friends, I often wondered, of course, whether they saw it in me. Had I changed that much physically? Had I changed much more than even I would allow myself to admit? I knew a fair amount of seniors who only seemed to socialize with people their age. And I, too, loved to spend time with some of my oldest friends. But I also treasured the time I was able to share with young people. They move more quickly and perceive things differently. Needless to say, they have quite a bit more energy. I always liked people with energy because it never failed to invigorate me. I certainly realized, after a while, that I had slowed down quite a bit. I could keep up pretty well if I had an arm to hold onto, but then can't everyone? I would see people running for the bus or dashing down the street, and I would think, *Did I ever do that?* But I dealt with it by admitting that I could do nothing about it. I would just have to go slower. But that didn't mean I had to stop moving.

I learned that life is such that if things will happen, they will happen. This probably sounds strange coming from a woman who devoted much of her life to battling for oppressed people's self-determination. I never particularly liked the idea of getting old, but I became something of a fatalist. So if I was in a hurry, for instance, I might cross a street amid busy traffic. If it was my turn to go, then it was my turn. In fact, I began to identify with a character in "The Fatalist," a short story by Isaac Bashevis Singer, the Nobel Prize–winning writer who happened to live across the street from me on Eighty-sixth Street. In the story, Benjamin Schwartz, who lived in a little shtetl, was madly in love with a woman, Heyele, who didn't want any part of him. He begged and pleaded and told her he would love her and care for her. Finally, he told her if she didn't want him, then he was going to lie down on the railroad tracks in front of an oncoming locomotive. "Do it," she said, certain that he wouldn't. But then he did. Fearing for his life, she tried to stop him as the train came roaring toward him, but he wouldn't budge. In the end, the train stopped inches from him. It wasn't his time.

I began to realize that, when it was my time, I didn't want a prolonged death. I didn't know whom to pray to—or, indeed, if any prayer is involved—but I hoped that it would happen rather quickly. Most all of the losses I've had of the people who were closest to me—my brother, my father, Charles, Andy, Bobby, Joe—were sudden. I hated the thought of ending up in the hospital for months with tubes keeping me alive. I feared being a nonperson living in a world of people. But until then, I vowed to go on, to achieve as much as possible in whatever remaining time the Fates allowed me.

I once asked a question of a slightly younger friend: "What do you do during the day?"

"Nothing," she told me, offering a few minor examples that bolstered her statement. "What's there to do?"

What's there to do? I would always wonder instead: Is there time to do everything?

Dr. Goodman at her desk,
age 90

REMEMBRANCE

$\mathcal{C}$arolyn Goodman passed away on August 17, 2007, at the age of ninety-one. Before she did so, in typical fashion, she carefully planned how she would be memorialized. She wrote specific instructions for her son, David, about how to run her memorial service. In charge as always, she planned her "Remembrance Celebration," which took place on October 7 at the New York Society for Ethical Culture, the same building where her son had been memorialized forty-three years earlier.

"This is the first time, since Jonny and I had kids, that our families have been together under the same roof at the same time," said David Goodman, opening the service. "Our mother arranged that." Carolyn also arranged to include speakers representing all facets of her personal, professional, and passionate

197

existence, asking them only to "limit their speaking to five minutes so that the celebration of my life isn't as long as my life."

New York City Mayor Michael Bloomberg spoke first, telling the six hundred attendees, "She taught the nation an unforgettable lesson—a lesson in personal strength and dignity in the face of unbearable suffering." U.S. Congressman and civil rights icon John Lewis marveled at how she "never, ever demonstrated one bit of bitterness or malice. . . . She worked with others, especially young people, to help build and inspire another generation not to give up. Because she never gave up."

Her colleagues in her many activist pursuits recalled her limitless energy for each cause. Edwin Goodman, formerly of the Pacifica Foundation, insisted, "If there is a heaven, Carolyn is there. But she doesn't see it as a perfect place. It clearly needs work." His former colleague Larry Josephson agreed, surmising that she is probably "organizing for better wages and shorter hours and to end discrimination by the angels."

Carolyn's friends in the New York media came out in force. Legendary newsman Gabe Pressman described her as "a woman of courage who passed her passion on to her son." Bob Herbert, columnist for *The New York Times,* celebrated "her decency and grace . . . her lifetime commitment to the worthiest but sometimes the most difficult causes." NY1 television host Budd Mishkin declared, "Tonight there are people all over the world . . . who might be facing difficult decisions—perhaps choosing between what's easy and what's right. If the decision is the path that is more unpopular, perhaps more dangerous, but more just . . . in those moments, Carolyn Goodman lives."

Voices from Mississippi were there, too. James Chaney's younger brother Ben declared, "The blessing that she left us is that when everything else fails, love remains . . . It bears all. It believes in all. It hopes for all. It endures all." Dick Molpus, the former Secretary of State, added, "We have learned from Carolyn Goodman. I don't mean to imply that we in Mississippi are where we need to be. There are men and women still gripped by the sickness of racial hatred, but those voices are slowly and steadily moving toward the darkness . . . So today we give praise and thanks specifically for Carolyn Goodman for a life that brought profound grace to a troubled land." And two young activists strode to the podium—Sarah Siegel and Allison Nichols, whose high school documentary helped spur at-long-last justice in Mississippi: "After meeting Dr. Goodman, activism was no longer just a theory. It was a lifestyle. And history was no longer confined to 'Once upon a time long ago . . .'"

Perhaps the most touching moment of the afternoon came when a clearly nervous but simply eloquent woman named Regina Solano admitted that she had managed to overcome her lifelong fear of public speaking in order to honor Carolyn, who was her strength and savior when she was part of the Parent and Child Education program at the Bronx Psychiatric Center.

"I was a very angry twenty-four-year-old single mother with two girls and one more on the way. Here was a woman who drove into PACE every morning in a new silver Volvo and sat with me with her hair swept up in a perfect bun like someone from the movies. I thought to myself, *What the hell could she possibly know about pain, anger, and fear? How dare she sit there and think she could help me,*" she said. "What did I learn from PACE? I began to learn how to be a mother."

The celebration came to a close, per Carolyn's wishes, with the audience clapping and singing "When the Saints Go Marching In." There were more smiles than tears.